CONTAINER
· Theme Gardens ·

CONTAINER
Theme Gardens

42
COMBINATIONS

EACH USING
5 perfectly matched plants

NANCY J. ONDRA

PHOTOGRAPHY BY ROB CARDILLO

Storey Publishing

The mission of Storey Publishing is to serve our customers by publishing practical information that encourages personal independence in harmony with the environment.

Edited by Carleen Madigan and Sarah Guare
Art direction and cover design by Jeff Stiefel
Indexed by Christine R. Lindemer, Boston Road Communications

Cover and interior photography by © Rob Cardillo
Photo styling by Nancy J. Ondra

Storey Publishing
210 MASS MoCA Way
North Adams, MA 01247
www.storey.com

Printed in China by R.R. Donnelley
10 9 8 7 6 5 4 3 2 1

Library of Congress Cataloging-in-Publication Data
Ondra, Nancy J., author.
  Container theme gardens : 42 combinations, each using 5 perfectly
  matched plants / Nancy J. Ondra.
     pages cm
  Includes bibliographical references and index.
  ISBN 978-1-61212-398-1 (pbk. : alk. paper)
  ISBN 978-1-61212-399-8 (ebook) 1. Container gardening. I. Title.
SB418.O63 2016
635.9'86—dc23
              2015031345

CONTENTS

Why Try CONTAINERS?

NO MATTER WHAT SIZE YARD YOU HAVE — or even if you have no yard at all — containers give you the opportunity to be a gardening star. Working with five plants gives you plenty of options for interesting color combinations and a diversity of plant forms: something upright, something trailing, and a few in-betweens to nicely fill out the middle. That's enough to create an entire garden in one spot, with no need for digging, mulching, or even weeding; no huge budget for buying dozens or hundreds of plants to get a good show; no worries about getting stuck with design or planting mistakes for years to come. Just add water (and some fertilizer now and then), and you can enjoy beautiful blooms and lush, lovely leaves even if you swear you've got the blackest thumb in the neighborhood.

Containers appeal to a wide range of people because they serve a wide range of purposes. For many folks, they're an aesthetic indulgence. In the same way that artwork and knick-knacks give an interior room a finished look, well-chosen container plantings can serve as design accessories around the outside of your home: by your front door, on a deck or patio, or around a pool. Or they can serve a simpler function: to give you a spot of color to brighten your day as you

head out the door in the morning or have a moment to sit down out back after dinner.

Well, color's great, but if that's all you're after, you could pop a bunch of silk flowers in a pot and not even need to water. So why container *plantings?* Living plants have so much more to offer than just color: for one thing, they change as they grow, marking the changing seasons and giving you a reason to keep watching them. They appeal to your other senses, too: you can enjoy sweet, flowery, or spicy scents; revel in the flavors of fresh-picked edibles; listen to rustling leaves and stems as they move in the breeze; and appreciate the soft touch of a fuzzy leaf or delicate petal on your skin. Living, growing plants also provide food and shelter for interesting creatures, such as songbirds, hummingbirds, butterflies, and moths, bringing them right up into your outdoor living space for easy observation. If you spend a good part of your week cooped up in an office, on the road, or stuck in your house, the opportunity to interact with a little bit of nature for a few minutes a day is a gift you can give yourself without guilt.

If you're more interested in the practical side of gardening in containers, there are plenty of excellent reasons to consider here as well.

NINE REASONS
to try
CONTAINERS

1 **PROVIDE IDEAL GROWING CONDITIONS.**
Containers make it much easier to supply the right conditions for the plants you want to grow. Simply tailor your watering routine to your plants and set your container in the right shady or sunny spot!

2 **SUPPLY PRIVACY.**
Plants are super for providing screening around a pool, patio, or other sitting area, but borders and hedges need a good bit of ground space and take several years to fill out. With a collection of containers, you can block the view of ugly eyesores, screen out nosy neighbors, and give exposed outdoor living spaces a sense of enclosure within just a few weeks.

3 **START RIGHT AWAY.**
If you're brand new to gardening, or if you've moved to a new place but have not yet had time to dig beds and borders, containers give you a place to play as soon as you like — no need to rush into landscape design decisions that may turn out to be a mistake later on.

4
CONTAIN YOUR EXPERIMENTS.
Want to try out a new plant or try out a color combination you've never used before? Pots and planters let you give plants and partnerships a test run before you commit to planting them in your garden.

5

CONTROL CREEPERS.

Some perennials, ornamental grasses, and ground covers are lovely to look at but scary-fast spreaders if you let them loose in your garden. When you plant them in containers — and keep them on a hard surface, so their creeping roots can't escape through the drainage holes — you can appreciate them without worry.

6

SAVE TIME AND MONEY.

For around $50 (or up to several hundred dollars, if you want a *really* nice pot), you can buy five plants that will give you months of pleasure and a container that you can use for several years — and all that will take up only a few square feet of space.

7

PAMPER TINY TREASURES.

A garden filled with lush, leafy plants is pretty to look at, but it can be a tough place for small-scale gems, such as succulents, alpines, and dainty woodland wildflowers, to compete with bigger plants. Give these little guys a container, though, and they'll grow happily with no worries about them getting smothered by more vigorous companions.

8

CREATE INSTANT IMPACT.

Need quick color for a backyard wedding, family reunion, or other special event? Fill a collection of containers with flowers and foliage to make your yard look amazing without the multi-year commitment of big in-ground gardens.

9

MAKE MAINTENANCE EASY.

Keep your containers close to an outdoor faucet and watering's hardly a chore. Containers are within easier reach for planting and grooming, too — ideal if you have limited mobility. Containers can also keep your plantings safe from rabbits, voles, and other small critters — possibly even deer, if you keep the pots close to your house.

BASICS OF CONTAINER GARDENING

REIN IT IN. Once a week or so, pinch or snip off fading flowers, damaged leaves, and stems that are outgrowing their space. If one plant is crowding out the others, prune out some of the biggest leaves or most vigorous stems.

PAIR LIKE WITH LIKE. Select plants with similar climate and site needs. Plants that need shade and those that demand lots of sun won't thrive together in the same planter. Succulents like this stonecrop, for example, prefer drier soil and full sun.

CHOOSE THE RIGHT SIZE CONTAINER. Small pots limit your plant choices, need more careful watering, and are more prone to getting knocked over. Larger pots are more expensive to fill, but they greatly expand your plant options. And because they hold more soil, they don't need to be watered as often.

LET THE WATER FLOW. Make sure your container has drainage holes. If it doesn't, you'll need to create some; it's easy to make holes in plastic, resin, and wooden planters. If your container doesn't have feet, like this one does, you'll need to raise the base of the pot an inch or so above the saucer, deck, or paving in order to prevent the drainage holes from becoming blocked.

Water enough to keep the potting soil from drying out but not so much that it stays soggy. Check the moisture level every other day, or every day in hot and dry weather.

Most soilless potting mixes will work fine for typical container combinations. Fertilize often with a liquid fertilizer. Check the label of the product you choose for specific instructions.

STEP-BY-STEP CONTAINER PLANTING

1. Moisten peat-based potting mixes before putting them in your container. In batches, combine the potting mix and water in a tub and knead the mix with your hands to distribute the moistened mix evenly.

2. Fill the planting container to about 4 inches below the rim with the moistened potting mix.

3. Before removing your plants from their original containers, make sure their rootballs are thoroughly moistened. Water until the excess runs out of the bottom of their pots. If they are very dry, give them a thorough soaking by submerging their pots in a bucket of water.

4. Remove your plants from their pots and put them in their new container. Scoop aside the potting soil or add more if needed, so the plants are sitting at about the same level they were in their original pots. Fill in around the rootballs with moistened potting soil, leaving some space between the rim of the pot and the top of the potting soil, so water or rain won't just run off the top.

5. Water the whole collection thoroughly to settle the potting soil around the roots and remove any large air pockets. Add more potting soil, if needed, to relevel the surface.

6. If you're starting with plants that have been growing in a greenhouse, expose them to outside conditions gradually — a process called hardening off. The greater the difference between greenhouse and outdoor conditions, the more careful you need to be.

FIVE-PART
Harmony of Color

IF COLOR IS YOUR PRIMARY INTEREST WHEN you're creating container combinations, playing with harmonies can be a fun way to focus your plant choices. This container is based on an "analogous" color scheme: in other words, colors that are next to each other on the color wheel, which goes from red to orange to yellow to green to blue to indigo to violet, and back around to red. Pick one dominant color — red, in this case — then a secondary color from one side or the other. I could have chosen orange, but I went with purples instead for this pot. These simple sorts of harmonies are easy to make and guaranteed to please.

FULL SUN TO PARTIAL SHADE

CONTAINER: 14" WIDE × 16" HIGH

PLANTS:

1 Japanese blood grass (*Imperata cylindrica* 'Rubra')

2 'Flamenco Samba' cuphea (*Cuphea llavea*)

3 DOLCE CINNAMON CURLS heuchera (*Heuchera* 'Inheuredfu')

4 Purple heart (*Setcreasea pallida*)

5 MINIFAMOUS DOUBLE RED calibrachoa (*Calibrachoa* 'Kleca13257')

The pot itself can play a major role in representing your color theme, as it does here.

1. JAPANESE BLOOD GRASS

Imperata cylindrica 'Rubra' | one 6-inch pot

ALTERNATES: Another 12- to 20-inch-tall, upright or spiky plant with rich red to near-black foliage, such as 'Eaton Canyon' fountain grass (*Pennisetum setaceum*), 'Black Pearl' pepper (*Capsicum annuum*), or 'Religious Radish' coleus (*Solenostemon scutellarioides*)

2. 'FLAMENCO SAMBA' CUPHEA

Cuphea llavea
one 4-inch pot

ALTERNATES: 'Flamenco Cha Cha' or 'Firefly' cuphea or another 8- to 12-inch-tall, bushy plant with red flowers, such as **BABYLON RED** verbena (*Verbena* 'Oxena'), 'Infinity Red' New Guinea impatiens (*Impatiens hawkeri*), or **SUPERTUNIA RED** petunia (*Petunia* 'Ustuni223')

4. PURPLE HEART

Setcreasea pallida
one 4-inch pot

ALTERNATES:
Another 6- to 10-inch-tall plant with deep purple foliage, such as **BLACK SCALLOP** ajuga (*Ajuga reptans* 'Binblasca'), **ILLUSION MIDNIGHT LACE** sweet potato vine (*Ipomoea batatas* 'Ncornsp011mnlc'), or **CHARMED WINE** oxalis (*Oxalis* 'Jroxburwi')

5. MINIFAMOUS DOUBLE RED CALIBRACHOA

Calibrachoa 'Kleca13257' | one 4-inch pot

ALTERNATES: **MINIFAMOUS COMPACT DARK RED** ('Kleca07145'), **SUPERBELLS RED** ('Uscali28'), or another calibrachoa with bright red flowers, or another 4- to 6-inch-tall, trailing plant in that color range, such as **SURFINIA RED** petunia (*Petunia* 'Sunremi')

3. DOLCE CINNAMON CURLS HEUCHERA

Heuchera 'Inheuredfu'
one 6-inch pot

ALTERNATES: 'Cajun Fire', 'Fire Alarm', or another heuchera with deep red to purple foliage, or another 6- to 10-inch-tall, bushy plant in that color range, such as bloodleaf (*Iresine herbstii*) or 'Wizard Velvet Red' coleus (*Solenostemon scutellarioides*)

FIVE-PART HARMONY of COLOR
season by season

SPRING

The primary color impact in spring comes from the container itself, along with the vivid red foliage of **DOLCE CINNAMON CURLS** heuchera and purely purple purple heart. You may also get a few flecks of early bloom on the 'Flamenco Samba' cuphea and **MINIFAMOUS DOUBLE RED** calibrachoa. Japanese blood grass tends to be a late riser, so it'll probably just be short green shoots at this time.

Get this container started once nighttime temperatures stay above 50°F/10°C (many of these plants are quite cold-tolerant, but the cuphea's growth may be stunted if it gets chilled). Once the plants are in place, water thoroughly to settle them into the potting soil.

EARLY TO MID SUMMER

As the weather warms up, so do the rich hues of this five-plant container. The purple-and-red blooms of 'Flamenco Samba' cuphea echo the leaves of both **DOLCE CINNAMON CURLS** heuchera and purple heart, as well as the dainty double flowers of **MINIFAMOUS DOUBLE RED** calibrachoa. The Japanese blood grass starts showing off now, too: mostly green, but beginning to blush red at the tips.

Water regularly to keep the potting soil evenly moist (but not soggy). Add a liquid fertilizer every 10 to 14 days as well, to encourage vigorous growth and lots of flowers. If necessary, clip off some of the older leaves of the heuchera to keep it from smothering the Japanese blood grass. The purple heart may produce pink flowers at the shoot tips, but they don't complement the others colors in this container, so trim them off.

TIDBITS TIPS AND TRICKS

OTHER COLORFUL VERTICALS. Adding some sort of spiky plant gives your container planting a vertical accent that contrasts nicely with mounded and trailing companions. Instead of going with the traditional green dracaena spike (*Dracaena*), consider an upright ornamental grass. For reds, also try 'Cheyenne Sky' switch grass (*Panicum virgatum*). For powder blues, consider blue wheat grass (*Elymus magellanicus*) or 'Heavy Metal' switch grass. Variegated 'Gold Bar' miscanthus (*Miscanthus sinensis*) adds a touch of yellow, while 'Morning Light' miscanthus is nice for a touch of white. Two green grasses that can be stars in their own right include Mexican feather grass (*Stipa tenuissima*) and corkscrew rush (*Juncus effusus* 'Spiralis').

MID TO LATE SUMMER

The harmony keeps humming through the summer months, with the various purples and reds all firing now to create a stunning display.

Continue with watering and fertilizing to support the lush growth and abundant blooms. Take a good look at the entire container every week or two and do whatever trimming is necessary to keep the plants in proportion to the container and to one another. Keep clipping off the flowers of the purple heart.

FALL

This profusion of reds and purples still looks lovely into autumn, with the Japanese blood grass reaching its best redness now to complement the colors of the other foliage and flowering plants.

Keep watering (but not fertilizing) as long as the plants are still growing and flowering. As the weather gets cold, the cuphea will bloom less and eventually get nipped by frost; once that happens, add the cuphea and calibrachoa to your compost pile. Pot up the purple heart and bring it indoors for the winter. The heuchera and Japanese blood grass are hardy in many areas (usually Zone 4 for the heuchera and Zone 5 or 6 for the grass), but they may have trouble settling in before winter from a mid-fall planting.

MORE COLOR COMBINATIONS. Looking for other options for pleasing color harmonies? If you'd like to stick with rich colors, consider bright red with clear orange, orange with sunny yellow, yellow-green with blue, or intense blue with purples. Or go the same route but with softer tints: pink with peach, apricot with butter yellow, soft yellow with baby blue, or cool blue with lavender-purple.

BOLD
Contrast

STRONG CONTRASTS ARE GUARANTEED attention-grabbers, making them a terrific theme for a container planting in an entryway or on a deck or patio where you do a lot of outdoor entertaining. There are lots of ways to create contrasts: by size, for instance, with one tall plant surrounded by carpeting and trailing plants, or with large leaves paired with tiny ones. Or, consider contrasting textures, such as spiky or grassy foliage with broad or lacy leaves or glossy leaves against fuzzy foliage. And then there are high-impact color contrasts, of course. This collection features rich reds and brilliant yellows, but there are plenty of other possibilities, such as blue or purple with orange or gold; or red, hot pink, or even black with white or silver.

FULL SUN

CONTAINER: 18" WIDE × 20" HIGH

PLANTS:

1 'Callie Bright Red' calibrachoa (*Calibrachoa*)

2 'Dancing Flame' scarlet sage (*Salvia splendens*)

3 'Goldfinger' sweet potato vine (*Ipomoea batatas*)

4 'Graffiti Bright Red' starflower (*Pentas lanceolata*)

5 LITTLE LUCKY POT OF GOLD lantana (*Lantana camara* 'Balucgold')

High-contrast plantings — particularly those based on color — give you a lot to look at, so it's best to stick with a simple container shape in a solid, dark shade, such as black, charcoal, or deep brown.

1. 'CALLIE BRIGHT RED' CALIBRACHOA

Calibrachoa
one 3- to 4-inch pot

ALTERNATES: **MINIFAMOUS VAMPIRE** ('Kleca09172') or **SUPERBELLS POMEGRANATE PUNCH** ('Uscal08501') calibrachoa, or another 4- to 6-inch-tall, semi-trailing plant with red flowers, such as 'Empress of India' nasturtium (*Tropaeolum majus*) or **SUN PARASOL GARDEN CRIMSON** mandevilla (*Mandevilla* 'Sunparacore')

2. 'DANCING FLAME' SCARLET SAGE

Salvia splendens | one 3- to 4-inch pot

ALTERNATES: 'Golden Delicious' pineapple sage (*Salvia elegans*) or another 2- to 3-foot-tall, upright plant with red or red-and-yellow flowers, such as 'Lucifer' canna (*Canna*), or with red or yellow foliage, such as **BIG RED JUDY** ('Uf06-40-01') or 'Redhead' coleus (*Solenostemon scutellarioides*)

3. 'GOLDFINGER' SWEET POTATO VINE

Ipomoea batatas | one 3- to 4-inch pot

ALTERNATES: 'Compact Margie' or 'Sweet Caroline
Light Green' sweet potato vine, or another 4- to 6-inch-tall,
yellow-leaved or yellow-variegated trailing plant, such as golden
hardy fuchsia (*Fuchsia magellanica* 'Aurea') or 'Walkabout
Sunset' dense-flowered loosestrife (*Lysimachia congestiflora*)

4. 'GRAFFITI BRIGHT RED' STARFLOWER

Pentas lanceolata | one 3- to 4-inch pot

ALTERNATES: 'New Look Red' starflower or another
12- to 18-inch-tall, bushy plant with bright red blooms, such
as **SUNPATIENS COMPACT RED** impatiens (*Impatiens*
'Sakimp024') or 'Gallery Singer' dahlia (*Dahlia*)

5. LITTLE LUCKY POT OF GOLD LANTANA

Lantana camara 'Balucgold' | one 3- to 4-inch pot

ALTERNATES: 'New Gold' lantana or another 6- to
12-inch-tall, bushy plant with yellow flowers, such as
'Lemon Gem' signet marigold (*Tagetes tenuifolia*) or
'Profusion Yellow' zinnia (*Zinnia*)

BOLD CONTRAST
season by season

You'll get a hint of the colors to come right from planting time, thanks to the yellow leaves of the 'Goldfinger' sweet potato vine and the yellow-specked foliage of 'Dancing Flame' scarlet sage, as well as whatever blooms are just beginning to open on the 'Callie Bright Red' calibrachoa, 'Graffiti Bright Red' starflower, and **LITTLE LUCKY POT OF GOLD** lantana.

Don't be in a hurry to get this container started, because some of these bright beauties (especially the sweet potato vine) can be stunted by cold weather. It's best to wait until nighttime temperatures are consistently at least 55°F/13°C before planting them outdoors. After planting, water regularly to encourage steady growth.

As the weather heats up, so does the color impact of this container, with bright new blooms on the 'Callie Bright Red' calibrachoa, 'Graffiti Bright Red' starflower, and **LITTLE LUCKY POT OF GOLD** lantana. The 'Dancing Flame' scarlet sage may have a few flowers now, but it's mostly contributing flashy foliage, as is the 'Goldfinger' sweet potato vine.

Keep up with watering, and add a dose of liquid fertilizer every week or two to support the abundance of new growth and developing flowers.

TIDBITS TIPS AND TRICKS

CONTRAST IN THE SHADE. For a similar high-impact contrast in a shady site, consider 'Nonstop Yellow' tuberous begonia (*Begonia* × *tuberhybrida*) and 'Gartenmeister Bonstedt' fuchsia (*Fuchsia triphylla*) for yellow and red flowers and golden creeping Jenny (*Lysimachia nummularia* 'Aurea'), 'Splash Select Red' polka-dot plant (*Hypoestes phyllostachya*), and 'Dipt in Wine' or 'Wasabi' coleus (*Solenostemon scutellarioides*) for red and yellow foliage.

COMPACT VINES. Sweet potato vines (*Ipomoea batatas*) are terrific trailers for foliage color in pots, planters, window boxes, and hanging baskets. Some of the older selections, such as 'Blackie' and 'Margarita', can be rather *too* vigorous, though, needing

Rousing reds from the 'Callie Bright Red' calibrachoa and 'Graffiti Bright Red' starflower and glowing gold from **LITTLE LUCKY POT OF GOLD** lantana are radiating with richness at this time of year, complemented by the bright yellow leaves of the 'Goldfinger' sweet potato vine. Toward the end of the summer, new flowers start forming at the shoot tips of 'Dancing Flame' scarlet sage; until then, the brightly variegated leaves keep looking great.

Regular watering and fertilizing are critical for maintaining all of the lush growth and flowers now. Clip off the bloom clusters of the starflower and lantana as soon as all of the blossoms drop, to encourage the plant to branch out and make more flowers. The sweet potato vine may need a harder pruning if it gets too enthusiastic: cut the vines back by half or more if they're getting overly long.

'Callie Bright Red' calibrachoa may be taking a bit of a break from flowering as fall begins, but it's usually back in bloom in early fall, especially if you kept up with summer fertilizing. It, along with the 'Graffiti Bright Red' starflower and **LITTLE LUCKY POT OF GOLD** lantana, will keep flowering through fall, right up to frost. 'Dancing Flame' scarlet sage bursts into bloom in early fall, contributing a spectacle of bright red flowers over the bushy clump of yellow-splashed leaves. 'Goldfinger' sweet potato continues to complete this red-and-yellow theme until zapped by frost.

Keep watering as long as the plants are growing, and continue with regular grooming, clipping or pinching off the flowers as they finish. Once the cold calls an end to the display, pull out the plants and add them to your compost pile.

regular trimming so they don't overwhelm their companions. To minimize maintenance — and get fuller-looking vines — look for series that have been selected for more compact growth, such as Desana, Illusion, Sweet Caroline, and Sweet Georgia.

TIDYING UP. Calibrachoa is usually "self-cleaning" — in other words, the old blooms drop off on their own — but it may benefit from a light trim in mid to late summer if the stems look straggly.

Pretty IN PASTEL

SOFT-COLOR CONTAINER COMBINATIONS are easy on the eye — and easy to put together, too, because you'll be able to find lots of beautiful flowers to work with. For a designer touch, start with a multicolored plant and play off its colors as you build the combination: choose a few complementary bloom colors for harmony and maybe one or two contrasting colors for a bit of drama. The 'Limon Blush' coleus inspired the rest of the plant choices, with the foliage or flowers of each one echoing the pink, yellow, purple, and greens in the coleus' leaves.

FULL SUN TO PARTIAL SHADE

CONTAINER: 15" WIDE × 12" HIGH

PLANTS:

1 'Summer Glow' hummingbird mint (*Agastache*)

2 'Limon Blush' coleus (*Solenostemon scutellarioides*)

3 Purple culinary sage (*Salvia officinalis* 'Purpurascens')

4 SUPERTUNIA FLAMINGO petunia (*Petunia* 'Bhtun6202')

5 'Scopia Great Regal Blue' bacopa (*Sutera cordata*)

1. 'SUMMER GLOW' HUMMINGBIRD MINT

Agastache | one 4-inch pot

ALTERNATES: 'Acapulco White and Yellow' hummingbird mint or another 12- to 18-inch-tall, upright, bushy plant with light yellow flowers or yellow-variegated foliage, such as 'Alligator Tears' coleus (*Solenostemon scutellarioides*), 'Golden Girl' autumn sage (*Salvia*), or variegated culinary sage (*S. officinalis* 'Icterina')

2. 'LIMON BLUSH' COLEUS

Solenostemon scutellarioides
one 4-inch pot

ALTERNATES:
Another 8- to 12-inch-tall, bushy plant with leaves or flowers in the soft yellow-peach-pink range, such as 'Landmark Pink Dawn', 'Landmark Peach Sunrise', or **LUCKY SUNRISE ROSE** ('Balandrise') lantana (*Lantana camara*); 'Lanai Peach' verbena (*Verbena*); or **SUNPATIENS COMPACT BLUSH PINK** impatiens (*Impatiens* 'Sakimp013')

3. PURPLE CULINARY SAGE

Salvia officinalis 'Purpurascens' | one 4-inch pot

ALTERNATES: Another 6- to 12-inch-tall, bushy or spiky plant with pastel purple or blue flowers, such as **ANGELFACE DRESDEN BLUE** *('Ansky')* or **ANGELFACE WEDGWOOD BLUE** ('Anwedgim') angelonia *(Angelonia),* or **CAPE TOWN BLUE** Felicia daisy *(Felicia* 'King Fisher')

4. SUPERTUNIA FLAMINGO PETUNIA

Petunia 'Bhtun6202' one 4-inch pot

ALTERNATES: 'Suncatcher Pink Lemonade', 'Crazytunia Terracotta', or another pastel pink or peach to soft yellow petunia, or another 4- to 8-inch-tall, trailing plant with pastel pink flowers, such as 'Aloha Kona Soft Pink' or **SUPERBELLS PEACH** *(*'Uscali671m') calibrachoa *(Calibrachoa)* or 'Mojave Pink' purslane *(Portulaca grandiflora)*

5. 'SCOPIA GREAT REGAL BLUE' BACOPA

Sutera cordata | one 4-inch pot

ALTERNATES: **SNOWSTORM BLUE** ('Danova886'), **SCOPIA GULLIVER BLUE** *(*'Dancop37'), or another light blue to lavender bacopa, or another 4- to 6-inch-tall, trailing plant with flowers in the same color range, such as **WHIRLWIND BLUE** fanflower *(Scaevola aemula* 'Scablhatis') or **SUPERBELLS MISS LILAC** calibrachoa *(Calibrachoa* 'Uscal87502')

PRETTY IN PASTEL
season by season

The 'Summer Glow' hummingbird mint will likely just be leafy at this point, but there's no lack of color in this pastel planter right from the start, thanks to the other flowers and foliage: a few early blooms on the **SUPERTUNIA FLAMINGO** petunia and 'Scopia Great Regal Blue' bacopa, and the leaves of the purple culinary sage and 'Limon Blush' coleus.

Wait until nighttime temperatures are at least 50°F/10°C to get this container started, so the coleus doesn't get stunted by cold. Once the plants are in place, water thoroughly to settle them into the potting soil.

Frilly-leaved 'Limon Blush' coleus and flower-filled **SUPERTUNIA FLAMINGO** petunia are the first plants to catch your eye right now, with the more muted purples of the purple culinary sage leaves and 'Scopia Great Regal Blue' bacopa adding their beauty when you see the container up close. 'Summer Glow' hummingbird mint will join the show around the end of this period, with creamy to peachy yellow blooms opening from soft gold buds.

Other than watering regularly (allowing the top inch or so of potting soil to dry out in between) and applying a liquid fertilizer every 10 to 14 days, there's not much more to do than enjoy the beauty of this pastel planting combination.

TIDBITS TIPS AND TRICKS

MORE APPEALING COMBINATIONS. Delicately tinted blossoms are just one part of a perfect pastel combination. Complement their pale colors with soft purple or yellow leaves, as in this combination, or try peachy pink, powder blue, or cool gray leaves. If you'd prefer your planter on the brighter side, include a plant or two with crisp white blooms or sparkling silver foliage instead. Or, create a touch of contrast with a dark-colored container or deep purple leaves to add a bit of intensity.

The 'Scopia Great Regal Blue' bacopa will probably take a bit of a break right now, but there's no lack of color through the hottest part of the summer, thanks to the abundant, spiky blooms of 'Summer Glow' hummingbird mint and lovely leaves of 'Limon Blush' coleus and purple culinary sage, as well as the **SUPERTUNIA FLAMINGO** petunia weaving through its companions.

Be sure to keep up with watering and fertilizing now to support the abundant growth and flowering. Take a good look at the whole container every week or so, and do a bit of clipping if any of the plants are crowding out their companions or growing out of proportion to the container. At some point during this time, consider giving the petunia an overall trim, cutting it back by about a third.

This collection of pretty-in-pastel plants will continue to look lovely well into fall. In fact, the flower colors may be a little richer now (though still on the soft side), due to the cooler temperatures.

Continue to water the plants as long as they're still growing. To help them last as long as possible, drape the container with a sheet at night or move it to a sheltered spot to get it through the first spell of light frosts. Once the cold kills the coleus, pull out all of the plants and add them to your compost pile, or plant the hummingbird mint and purple culinary sage in your garden, if you wish. (North of Zone 6, pot up both of these perennials and keep them in a cool, bright place for the winter.)

FORGOING FADING. Pastel flowers and foliage can work fine in full sun in cooler climates, but in intense sun and heat those delicate hues can quickly bleach out to near white, or scorch to brown. If your pastel blooms are getting lighter than you'd like, or if they're finishing too fast, try moving their pot to a spot with morning sun and afternoon shade, or at least a few hours of shade during the hottest part of the day.

Rich REDS

A SCARCITY OF SUNSHINE DOESN'T MEAN that you can't enjoy an abundance of color in your container combinations. Pairing prettily patterned foliage with plants that can bloom even without all-day sun is the perfect recipe for stunning shady containers. As vibrant as reds can be in sun-drenched sites, they tend to be more muted in shade, so you'll want to place a container like this where you can see it up close: on a north-facing deck, for instance, or next to a bench under your favorite backyard shade tree.

PARTIAL TO FULL SHADE

CONTAINER: 20" WIDE × 20" HIGH

PLANTS:

1 BIG RED JUDY coleus (*Solenostemon scutellarioides* 'Uf06-40-01')

2 DRAGON WING RED begonia (*Begonia* 'Bepared')

3 'Freida Hemple' caladium (*Caladium*)

4 'Red Dragon' fleeceflower (*Persicaria microcephala*)

5 'Splash Select Red' polka-dot plant (*Hypoestes phyllostachya*)

Let a few of the 'Red Dragon' fleeceflower stems trail over the side of the pot, if you like, or weave them among the coleus shoots to encourage them to grow upward instead.

1. BIG RED JUDY COLEUS

Solenostemon scutellarioides 'Uf06-40-01' | one 3- to 4-inch pot

ALTERNATES: 'Redhead' or another upright, red-leaved coleus, or an 18- to 24-inch-tall, red-leaved Japanese maple (*Acer palmatum*), such as 'Bloodgood' or 'Shaina'

2. DRAGON WING RED BEGONIA

Begonia 'Bepared' one 3- to 4-inch pot

ALTERNATES: 'Big Red with Green Leaf' begonia (*B.* × *benariensis*) or 'Nonstop Deep Red' tuberous begonia (*B.* × *tuberhybrida*), or a red-flowered New Guinea impatiens (*Impatiens hawkeri*), such as 'Harmony Red Cardinal'

3. 'FREIDA HEMPLE' CALADIUM

Caladium | one 4- to 6-inch pot

ALTERNATES: 'Florida Cardinal', 'Red Flash',
or another caladium with red leaf markings, or a rex begonia
(*Begonia rex*) with red leaves, such as 'Harmony's Red Robin'

4. 'RED DRAGON' FLEECE-FLOWER

Persicaria microcephala
one 6- to 8-inch pot

ALTERNATES:
'Dragon's Eye' fleece-flower, or a trailing coleus (*Solenostemon scutellarioides*) with red leaves, such as 'Trailing Red'

5. 'SPLASH SELECT RED' POLKA-DOT PLANT

Hypoestes phyllostachya | one 4- to 6-inch pot

ALTERNATES: 'Confetti Red' polka-dot plant or
'Brilliantissima' or 'Red Heart' bloodleaf (*Iresine herbstii*)

RICH REDS
season by season

This shady container collection offers color right from planting time, thanks to all of the lovely leaves: rich red **BIG RED JUDY** coleus, red-and-green 'Freida Hemple' caladium and 'Splash Select Red' polka-dot plant, and red-and-silver 'Red Dragon' fleeceflower, with a contrasting dash of bright and glossy green from the **DRAGON WING RED** begonia.

Wait until nighttime temperatures are consistently at least 60°F/15°C before getting this container started, so the plants don't get stunted by the cold. Keep the soil evenly moist (but not soggy) to help them settle in and produce lots of new growth. You may want to give them a dose of liquid fertilizer a week or two after planting to get them off to a good start. If the coleus has just one stem, pinch out the top ½ to 1 inch to encourage branching.

As the weather warms up and these plants fill out, their foliage display just keeps getting better and better, with the added bonus of the first of what will be many bright red blooms on the **DRAGON WING RED** begonia.

Regular watering, along with a dose of liquid fertilizer every 2 weeks or so, will keep these plants in top form. If the coleus is growing quickly and looks out of proportion to the other plants, cut one or two of the tallest stems back by a half to two-thirds to slow it down and shape it up a bit.

TIDBITS TIPS AND TRICKS

FUN WITH POLKA-DOT PLANT COLORS. Fortunately for container gardeners, polka-dot plants (*Hypoestes phyllostachya*) are getting easier to find — look in the indoor-plant area as well as bedding annual displays at your favorite greenhouse or garden center — but it can be hard to decide between the white-, pink-, rose-, and red-spotted forms. So, why choose at all? Buy a packet of 'Splash Select Mix' seeds from a mail-order source (or locally, if you can find it) and sow them indoors, in a warm, bright place, in early to mid spring. When the seedlings appear, you'll be able to tell their colors almost right away. Pot them up individually once they're 1 to 2 inches tall, and you'll have plenty of each color to play with in your pots and in your garden once all danger of frost has passed.

MID TO LATE SUMMER

By midsummer, the 'Freida Hemple' caladium and 'Splash Select Red' polka-dot plant are loaded with showy red-and-green leaves. The polka-dot plant also produces small, purplish pink flowers, but they're mostly hidden and won't detract from the overall red theme. **BIG RED JUDY** coleus, which tends to stay solid red in sunny sites, will often produce some greenish stippling and spots in shade. The leaves of 'Red Dragon' fleeceflower also change colors as the season progresses, from red-and-silver shoot tips to younger leaves that are red, silver, and green and silver-and-green older leaves. Through this period, the **DRAGON WING RED** begonia keeps producing loads of bright green leaves and clusters of brilliant red blooms.

Keep up with watering now — it takes a good bit of moisture to support all those lovely leaves — and fertilize every 10 to 14 days. A weekly grooming will also help to keep the whole collection looking its best.

FALL

This red grouping should stay beautiful into early fall, at least. The 'Freida Hemple' caladium will likely be the first to start declining, followed by the polka-dot plant; the rest usually keep looking good until frost, if you leave the container outdoors.

Keep watering regularly if you want to enjoy this container planting as long as possible. Once the plants have gotten nipped by frost, pull them out and toss them on your compost pile or try overwintering them. Take cuttings of the coleus and begonia, and dig out and pot up the polka-dot plant in early fall, and keep them on a sunny windowsill. Let the caladium bulb dry and store it at 55 to 60°F/13 to 15°C. 'Red Dragon' fleeceflower is normally winter-hardy as far north as Zone 4 or 5, but it likely won't make it there from a fall planting.

SUN-LOVING REDS. Need reds for sun instead? There are loads of rich red flowers to choose from for gorgeous containers. A collection of all-red flowers could be a bit overwhelming, though, so it's important to include some well-chosen foliage to separate the blooming plants a bit and let the different flowers show off to advantage. For a really smoldering five-plant combination, try three red bloomers with two partners that have deep purple to near black leaves, such as 'Black Pearl' pepper (*Capsicum annuum*) and 'Sweet Caroline Raven' sweet potato vine (*Ipomoea batatas*). Or, go for a high-contrast effect by combining rich red blossoms with bright silver foliage, such as 'Parfum d'Ethiopia' wormwood (*Artemisia*) and 'Silver Falls' silver ponyfoot (*Dichondra argentea*).

ORANGE
All Over

ORANGE MAY NOT BE A COLOR THEME THAT first comes to mind when you're planning a container, but it's certainly worth considering for its many intriguing combination possibilities. Think of how good the terra-cotta color of clay pots or the natural warmth of wood looks with a wide range of greens, and then bring those colors up into the plant layer. Go with bright, clear orange flowers and gold-orange foliage for a lively, sun-bright display or explore the softer option of peachy petals and coppery to bronzy leaves, as in this rectangular cedar planter, for a more calming combination.

FULL SUN TO PARTIAL SHADE

CONTAINER: 24" LONG × 12" WIDE × 12" HIGH

PLANTS:

1 'ColorBlaze Sedona' coleus (*Solenostemon scutellarioides*)

2 Coppertone stonecrop (*Sedum nussbaumerianum*)

3 MINIFAMOUS ORANGE calibrachoa (*Calibrachoa* 'Kleca11227')

4 'Profusion Deep Apricot' zinnia (*Zinnia*)

5 'Toffee Twist' sedge (*Carex flagellifera*)

Coppery to bronzy beauties, such as 'Toffee Twist' sedge, create intriguing effects when paired with bright orange blooms.

33

THE 5-PLANT PALETTE

1. 'COLORBLAZE SEDONA' COLEUS

Solenostemon scutellarioides | one 3- to 4-inch pot

ALTERNATES: 'ColorBlaze Keystone Kopper', 'Trusty Rusty', or another orange-leaved coleus, or another 12- to 18-inch-tall, bushy plant with orangey leaves or flowers, such as **ACAPULCO ORANGE** hummingbird mint (*Agastache mexicana* 'Kiegador')

2. COPPERTONE STONECROP

Sedum nussbaumerianum | one 3- to 4-inch pot

ALTERNATES: Another 4- to 6-inch-tall, bushy or trailing plant with orangey leaves or flowers, such as 'Mandarin Orange' or 'Sprite Orange' creeping zinnia (*Sanvitalia procumbens*) or 'Wildcat Mandarin' pimpernel (*Anagallis*)

3. MINIFAMOUS ORANGE CALIBRACHOA

Calibrachoa 'Kleca11227'
one 3- to 4-inch pot

ALTERNATES:
'Callie Orange',
**SUPERBELLS
DREAMSICLE**
('Uscali4117'), or
another orange
calibrachoa, or another
6- to 8-inch-tall, bushy
or trailing plant with
peachy orange flowers,
such as 'Caribbean
Crush' nasturtium
(*Tropaeolum majus*)

4. 'PROFUSION DEEP APRICOT' ZINNIA

Zinnia
two 3- to 4-inch pots

ALTERNATES:
Another 8- to 12-inch-tall,
bushy plant with orange
foliage or flowers, such
as firesticks (*Euphorbia
tirucalli*) or 'Figaro
Orange Shade' or 'Gallery
Vincent' dahlia (*Dahlia*)

5. 'TOFFEE TWIST' SEDGE

Carex flagellifera | one 4- to 6-inch pot

ALTERNATES: 'Bronze' New Zealand hair sedge
(*C. comans*), orange sedge (*C. testacea*), or another 8- to
12-inch-tall, mounded plant with orangey foliage, such as
DOLCE CRÈME BRULEE ('Tnheu042') or 'Marmalade'
heuchera (*Heuchera*)

ORANGE ALL OVER
season by season

This orange-all-over container offers some color right from planting time, mostly thanks to the foliage. 'ColorBlaze Sedona' coleus tends to be a rich orange at the start of the growing season, while coppertone sedum has orangey yellow leaves with deeper orange tips and 'Toffee Twist' sedge is coppery brown. It's not unusual to have a bloom or two (or a few) on the **MINIFAMOUS ORANGE** calibrachoa and 'Profusion Deep Apricot' zinnia, too, at planting time.

Hold off on planting until nighttime temperatures are consistently at least 55°F/13°C. (Most of these plants can tolerate cooler temperatures, but coleus tends to be touchy about the cold and may get stunted for a bit if it gets chilled.) If the coleus has just one stem, pinch out the top inch or so to encourage branching. Water enough to keep the potting soil moist, but let the top inch or so dry out between waterings.

MINIFAMOUS ORANGE calibrachoa and 'Profusion Deep Apricot' zinnia are contributing many more flowers now. The blooms tend to be more orangey when the weather is on the cooler side and a softer peachy color as the days heat up. Full sun keeps the most orangey color on the coppertone sedum, while 'ColorBlaze Sedona' coleus can take on a range of sunset shades, from orange to rich copper to nearly brick red, depending on the temperature and the amount of sunlight it gets. 'Toffee Twist' sedge tends to have an overall coppery cast through this time, while it's still putting on lots of new growth.

Water regularly, remembering to let the top inch of potting soil dry before watering again, because the calibrachoa and the sedum, in particular, can be prone to rot if the soil stays too moist. Apply a liquid fertilizer every 2 weeks. Pinch or clip off the old flowers on the zinnia plants.

TIDBITS TIPS AND TRICKS

MORE CONTAINERS FOR ORANGE BLOOMS. The container you choose for your orange-theme planting has a big influence on its visual impact. Yellow, too, complements orange, but the shade you choose makes a big difference: a pastel yellow pot pairs perfectly with peachy oranges, while a greenish yellow or bright yellow pot planted with glowing oranges is guaranteed to grab anyone's attention. For something really dramatic, pair bright orange bloomers with a brilliant blue–glazed container to create a high-contrast combination.

BROWN BEAUTIES. Brown leaves are usually a bad thing, but there are some really cool plants that have brown leaves even when they're perfectly healthy. 'Sweet Caroline Bronze' and 'Sweet Georgia Bronze' sweet potato vines (*Ipomoea batatas*) typically have a trailing habit but can also weave up through taller companions. Depending on the age of the leaves and the

MID TO LATE SUMMER

"Orange all over" definitely describes this container collection as the summer progresses and the flowers and foliage just keep coming. As in early to mid summer, the exact shades of orange to peach will vary depending on the light and weather, but however they turn out, you'll have no doubt about the color theme.

Maintain the watering and fertilizing routine through the rest of the summer. If the calibrachoa starts to bloom less or looks a bit straggly, cut it back by about a third to encourage new shoots and lots more flowers. You might also want to trim back the zinnia and coleus a bit to keep them well branched and in proportion to the rest of the container.

FALL

The colors keep changing as cooler autumn temperatures bring out different intensities in the orange shades of flowers and foliage, but it's still an orange container, for sure, and it will continue to look good until frost.

Keep up with the watering routine as long as the plants are actively growing, and do a little grooming and trimming as needed so the collection stays balanced and tidy-looking. The coleus will probably be the first plant to decline as cold weather returns. Once frost calls a halt to the growing season, pull out the calibrachoa, coleus, and zinnia and add them to your compost pile. Coppertone sedum is usually hardy in Zone 9 and areas south, but it can adapt well to life as a houseplant for the winter. You can keep 'Toffee Twist' sedge, too: in Zone 7 and south, plant it out in your garden when you dismantle the rest of the container.

amount of sunlight they get, their color can range from soft peach to light tan to rich chestnut to earthy raw umber. Various species and selections of New Zealand sedges (*Carex*) are also excellent choices for pinkish, orangey, or reddish browns: in a mounded form on 'Bronze' sedge (*C. comans*) and 'Toffee Twist' sedge (*C. flagellifera*) or upright on 'Red Rooster' and 'Red Fox' leatherleaf sedge (*C. buchananii*).

ORANGE PLANTS FOR SHADE. Oranges are most abundant for sunny sites, but there are also some outstanding orange-hued plants for shady containers. For flowers, consider 'Orange Marmalade' firecracker flower (*Crossandra infundibuliformis*) or orange-flowered begonias (*Begonia*), such as dainty 'Sparks Will Fly' or bold 'Nonstop Mocca Deep Orange' (*B. × tuberhybrida*). For orangey leaves, look for 'Prince of Orange' philodendron (*Philodendron*), autumn fern (*Dryopteris erythrosora*), or 'Sweet Tea' foamy bells (× *Heucherella*).

GROWING
Sunshine

FROM INTENSE ORANGEY GOLD TO CLEAR lemon to pale cream, yellow flowers have a cheery attitude that can brighten even a dreary day. Their sunny beauty is sure to draw attention, so a yellow-theme container is a great choice for dressing up a doorway, a set of steps, or a garden gate. This lime-green glazed pot holds a collection of bright yellow bloomers paired with chartreuse and yellow-variegated leaves for wonderfully welcome color from spring to frost.

FULL SUN TO LIGHT SHADE

CONTAINER: 12" WIDE × 12" HIGH

PLANTS:

1 'Figaro Yellow Shades' dahlia (*Dahlia*)

2 'Goldcrest' Monterey cypress (*Cupressus macrocarpa*)

3 Variegated culinary sage (*Salvia officinalis* 'Icterina')

4 'Illumination' lesser periwinkle (*Vinca minor*)

5 MINIFAMOUS COMPACT SAFRAN calibrachoa (*Calibrachoa* 'Kleca06098')

Avoid yellow overload by choosing one or two strong shades of yellow, a clear yellow, and one or two creamy or greenish yellows to give your container combination some visual variety.

39

1. 'FIGARO YELLOW SHADES' DAHLIA

Dahlia | one 3- to 4-inch pot

ALTERNATES: 'Dahlietta Julia' or 'Gallery Cezanne' dahlia, or another 6- to 12-inch-tall, bushy plant with bright yellow flowers, such as 'Profusion Yellow' zinnia (*Zinnia*)

2. 'GOLDCREST' MONTEREY CYPRESS

Cupressus macrocarpa | one 12- to 18-inch-tall plant

ALTERNATES: Another 12- to 18-inch-tall, upright plant with yellow foliage, such as 'Gold Cone' juniper (*Juniperus communis*), **MELLOW YELLOW** spirea (*Spiraea thunbergii* 'Ogon'), or 'Wasabi' coleus (*Solenostemon scutellarioides*)

3. VARIEGATED CULINARY SAGE

Salvia officinalis 'Icterina'
one 3- to 4-inch pot

ALTERNATES: Another 8- to 12-inch-tall, bushy plant with yellow-and-green foliage, such as variegated lemon thyme (*Thymus × citriodorus* 'Variegata') or variegated lilyturf (*Liriope muscari* 'Variegata')

4. 'ILLUMINATION' LESSER PERIWINKLE

Vinca minor | one 3- to 4-inch pot

ALTERNATES: Another 1- to 3-inch-tall, trailing plant with green-and-yellow or solid yellow foliage, such as golden creeping Jenny (*Lysimachia nummularia* 'Aurea') or 'Angelina' sedum (*Sedum rupestre*)

5. MINIFAMOUS COMPACT SAFRAN CALIBRACHOA

Calibrachoa 'Kleca06098' | one 3- to 4-inch pot

ALTERNATES: 'Catwalk Perfect Yellow' or **SUPERBELLS YELLOW** ('Uscal53002') calibrachoa or another 6- to 8-inch-tall, bushy to somewhat trailing plant with clear yellow flowers, such as **NAMID COMPACT YELLOW** bidens (*Bidens ferulifolia* 'Klebf07570')

GROWING SUNSHINE
season by season

The first color impact from this container collection comes mostly from the foliage: bright greenish yellow from the 'Goldcrest' Monterey cypress and yellow and green from the variegated culinary sage and 'Illumination' lesser periwinkle. There might also be a few clear yellow blooms on the 'Figaro Yellow Shades' dahlia and **MINIFAMOUS COMPACT SAFRAN** calibrachoa, and perhaps a few purple-blue flowers on the 'Illumination' periwinkle, around planting time.

All five of these plants tolerate a fair bit of cold, so you could get this container started as soon as there's no more chance of nighttime frosts, as long as the plants are all adapted to outdoor conditions and not straight out of a greenhouse. (If they *are* used to sheltered, warm, indoor conditions, expose them to gradually longer periods outside over the course of a week or so before planting the container.) Water lightly after planting.

There's no doubt about this container being a vision in yellow by now: the 'Goldcrest' Monterey cypress, variegated culinary sage, and 'Illumination' lesser periwinkle just keep getting leafier, and the 'Figaro Yellow Shades' dahlia and **MINIFAMOUS COMPACT SAFRAN** calibrachoa are producing lots of bright new blooms.

Regular watering is important for keeping the plants growing happily, but it's a good idea to let the top inch or two of soil dry out in between, because the calibrachoa can be prone to rot if the potting soil stays constantly moist. Use a liquid fertilizer every 2 weeks or so.

TIDBITS TIPS AND TRICKS

MORE GOLD! Want to go for gold on a grand scale? Fill a large planter with sizable annuals, perennials, tropicals, ornamental grasses, and shrubs with yellow, long-blooming flowers or yellow-variegated foliage, such as 'Landmark Yellow' lantana (*Lantana camara*), 'Margarita' sweet potato vine (*Ipomoea batatas*), 'Full Moon' coreopsis (*Coreopsis*), 'Gold Sword' yucca (*Yucca filamentosa*), 'Prairie Sun' black-eyed Susan (*Rudbeckia hirta*), 'Gold Bar' miscanthus (*Miscanthus sinensis*), and 'Sunburst' St. John's wort (*Hypericum frondosum*) — to name just a few.

YELLOW PLANTS FOR SHADY SITES. Sunny yellow blooms would be a lovely sight in shady sites, but there aren't many easy-to-find long-bloomers to choose

'Figaro Yellow Shades' dahlia and **MINIFAMOUS COMPACT SAFRAN** calibrachoa may take a bit of a break during the hottest part of the summer, but they usually still have a few flowers at any given time, and the 'Goldcrest' Monterey cypress, variegated culinary sage, and 'Illumination' lesser periwinkle continue to contribute colorful foliage through the rest of the season.

Maintain the watering routine through the rest of the summer, and fertilize again once or twice, stopping by late summer if you plan to leave any of the plants outdoors for the winter. Remove any of the dahlia flowers that are past their prime, and any leaves that are dead or damaged on any of the plants. If the calibrachoa starts blooming less, cut the plant back by a third to a half to encourage new growth and fresh flowers.

'Figaro Yellow Shades' dahlia and **MINIFAMOUS COMPACT SAFRAN** calibrachoa continue to bloom into fall, until they get zapped by freezing temperatures. 'Goldcrest' Monterey cypress, variegated culinary sage, and 'Illumination' lesser periwinkle all tolerate a fair bit of cold, so their beauty will carry on well after their flowering partners are done.

If you want to enjoy the container as long as possible, keep watering as long as the plants look good, then dismantle the collection in mid to late fall. Compost all of the plants if you plan to start fresh next year; that's usually the simplest route for the calibrachoa and dahlia, anyway. It's pretty easy to keep the Monterey cypress, sage, and periwinkle through the winter if you pot them up and keep them indoors in a cool, bright place.

from for partial to full shade: mostly tuberous begonias (*Begonia* × *tuberhybrida*), such as 'Nonstop Yellow', and wishbone flowers (*Torenia fournieri*), such as 'Kauai Lemon Drop'. You can still enjoy a wealth of lovely yellows, though, thanks to the many annuals and perennials with leaves that are striped, streaked, spotted, or splotched with yellow, or even solid gold: enough to make endless five-plant container combinations. For spiky or slender leaves, consider ornamental grasses such as variegated or 'All Gold' Hakone grass (*Hakonechloa macra*) or 'Banana Boat' broadleaf sedge (*Carex siderosticha*); for broad and bold, choose from among the many hundreds of yellow or yellow-variegated hostas (*Hosta*). Coleus (*Solenostemon scutellarioides*), too, come in an amazing array of leaf shapes and sizes to grace any shady container.

Singin' THE Blues

A CONTAINER COLLECTION BASED ON beautiful shades of blues adds a touch of class to any site. There are loads of pretty plants that fall into this category, but many "blue" flowers are actually more on the purple side, which is fine if that's what you like and what looks good in your chosen container. But for a container that's in a class by itself, consider a combination of true-blue blooms paired with rich green and cool powder-blue leaves. Prime time for this particular collection is late summer through fall. Thanks to the intense cobalt blue of the container itself, though, there's no doubt about the color theme regardless of the season.

FULL SUN TO LIGHT SHADE

CONTAINER: 12" WIDE × 12" HIGH

PLANTS:

1 Blue finger (*Senecio mandraliscae*)

2 'Blue Daze' evolvulus (*Evolvulus glomeratus*)

3 'Patio Deep Blue' gentian sage (*Salvia patens*)

4 Tweedia (*Tweedia caerulea*)

5 'Wildcat Blue' blue pimpernel (*Anagallis monelli*)

To help your blues stand out, pair them with partners that have silvery, gray, or white-variegated leaves.

45

1. BLUE FINGER

Senecio mandraliscae | one 3- to 4-inch pot

ALTERNATES: Another bushy, 6- to 8-inch-tall plant with spiky, powder-blue foliage, such as succulent blue chalk sticks (*Senecio serpens*) or 'Siskiyou Blue' blue fescue (*Festuca idahoensis*)

2. 'BLUE DAZE' EVOLVULUS

Evolvulus glomeratus | one 3- to 4-inch pot

ALTERNATES: 'Hawaiian Blue Eyes' evolvulus or another 4- to 6-inch-tall, bushy to semi-trailing plant with blue flowers, such as 'Cape Town Blue' blue daisy (*Felicia*) or compact ground morning glory (*Convolvulus sabatius* 'Compacta')

3. 'PATIO DEEP BLUE' GENTIAN SAGE

Salvia patens
one 3- to 4-inch pot

ALTERNATES: 'Guanajuato' gentian sage, or another upright, 12- to 18-inch-tall plant with spiky blue flowers, such as 'Cathedral Deep Blue' mealycup sage (*Salvia farinacea*)

4. TWEEDIA

Tweedia caerulea | one 3- to 4-inch pot

ALTERNATES: Another upright, 10- to 16-inch-tall plant with blue flowers, such as 'Blue Lady' bush violet (*Browallia americana*) or **ROYAL CAPE** cape leadwort (*Plumbago auriculata* 'Monott')

5. 'WILDCAT BLUE' BLUE PIMPERNEL

Anagallis monelli
one 3- to 4-inch pot

ALTERNATES: 'Angie Blue' or 'Gentian Blue' blue pimpernel, or another compact, trailing plant with blue flowers, such as leadwort (*Ceratostigma plumbaginoides*) or 'Techno Blue' blue lobelia (*Lobelia erinus*)

SINGIN' THE BLUES
season by season

The primary source of color early in the growing season comes from the container itself, plus the powder-blue, pointy foliage of blue finger and possibly a few early, gentian-blue blooms on the 'Wildcat Blue' blue pimpernel.

Wait until nighttime temperatures dependably stay above 45°F/7°C before putting these plants together in the container. Water thoroughly after planting, then as needed each time the top ½ to 1 inch of potting soil dries out.

'Wildcat Blue' blue pimpernel starts blooming in earnest now, joined by the slightly lighter but still distinctly blue 'Blue Daze' evolvulus. (Each of the evolvulus flowers lasts just one day, opening in the morning and closing in the afternoon, but the plant produces lots of new buds to keep the show going.) The cool blue leaves of blue finger, along with the silvery green foliage of the evolvulus and the hairy, gray-green leaves of tweedia, provide an interesting contrast to the intense blue of the blue pimpernel and evolvulus flowers and rich green of the gentian sage and blue pimpernel leaves.

Keep watering regularly, and add a liquid fertilizer every 7 to 10 days to encourage steady growth and flowering. Pinch out the top 1 inch or so of the shoot tips on the evolvulus, gentian sage, and tweedia to encourage bushier growth.

TIDBITS TIPS AND TRICKS

TRUE BLUE. When it comes to choosing blue flowers, don't be tricked by the names of the plants, or even by their pictures in a catalog or on a pot tag. Apart from all of the various tints and shades that are clearly more purple than blue, you'd be amazed at what some plant producers and seed companies try to pass off as blue: pale lavender, grayish purple, and even blues so light that they're practically white. Websites and catalogs may intensify the color of the blue flowers they show to make them more appealing, and to be fair, even the best-intentioned photographer may have trouble capturing the true shade of blue depending on the intensity and angle of sunlight. When you're absolutely determined to get perfectly coordinated blues for your five-plant container, make sure you see them in flower for yourself.

MID TO LATE SUMMER

This collection really comes into its own around now, as the 'Wildcat Blue' blue pimpernel and 'Blue Daze' evolvulus are joined by the cerulean blue stars of tweedia by midsummer and pure blue blooms of 'Patio Deep Blue' gentian sage by late summer. The pale blue foliage of blue finger completes the theme and adds a welcome bit of contrast to the intense flower colors.

Continue watering and fertilizing through the rest of the summer. Most of the plants neatly drop their dead flowers; keep those swept up, and remove any dead or damaged leaves. The blue finger may want to produce stalks topped with fuzzy white flowers now, but the blooms don't add to the blue theme, so it's best to keep them pinched or clipped off. Cut the bloom clusters off the tweedia as the flowers drop to keep the plant's energy directed into producing more blossoms instead of seedpods.

FALL

'Wildcat Blue' blue pimpernel and 'Blue Daze' evolvulus usually keep flowering until frost. Tweedia tends to produce a few new flowers into early fall, while 'Patio Deep Blue' gentian sage reaches its peak of beauty during these cooler days. Blue finger continues to add foliage color until freezing weather returns.

Stop fertilizing by early fall, but continue watering as long as the plants are still looking good. (Clip off any dead or damaged leaves, and any empty flower spikes on the gentian sage, to maintain the collection's good looks as long as possible.) If you want to keep the blue finger for next year, dig it out of the container before frost, pot it up, and keep it on a sunny windowsill for the winter. When a frost or freeze calls an end to the growing season, pull the rest of the plants out of the container and add them to your compost pile.

LEAFY "BLUE." If you're fairly new to gardening, you may be surprised when you see what gardeners mean when they use "blue" to describe leaves. We're not talking purple-blues here, as in petals, but rather green foliage heavily covered with a powdery or waxy coating that makes it look bluish gray or bluish green. Most intense on the new growth, these coatings may wear off as the growing season progresses, leaving the leaves looking more green than blue by the end of the summer. The oils on your hands can damage the blues as well, so handle the plants carefully at planting time and try not to touch them once they're in place.

Regal PURPLE

RICH PURPLE PETALS PAIRED WITH sumptuous purple foliage never fail to make an unforgettable impression: just the thing to add a touch of elegance to a front entry or dress up a deck. There are so many beautiful purple plants to choose from that it can be hard to limit yourself to just five. It helps to remember that when you stick with a limited color theme, you need to also have some variety in the form of different flower shapes and leaf textures: some spiky blooms and some rounded ones, and both big and little leaves. This lavish purple grouping is featured in a pale, urn-shaped pedestal planter that complements the height of taller plants and gives plenty of space for the lower-growing ones to trail over the sides.

FULL SUN TO PARTIAL SHADE

CONTAINER: 20" WIDE × 24" HIGH

PLANTS:

1 'Angelina Dark Purple' angelonia (*Angelonia angustifolia*)

2 'Marine' heliotrope (*Heliotropium arborescens*)

3 Persian shield (*Strobilanthes dyerianus*)

4 Purple heart (*Setcreasea pallida*)

5 SUPERBELLS GRAPE PUNCH calibrachoa (*Calibrachoa* 'Uscal84704')

Purple heart, also known as purple queen, is a great choice when you need bold purple foliage for a container combination.

THE 5-PLANT PALETTE

1. 'ANGELINA DARK PURPLE' ANGELONIA

Angelonia angustifolia | two 4-inch pots

ALTERNATES: **ANGELFACE BLUE IMPROVED** ('Anbluim') or 'Serena Purple' angelonia or another 12- to 18-inch-tall plant with spiky purple flowers, such as 'Evolution Violet' mealycup sage (*Salvia farinacea*)

2. 'MARINE' HELIOTROPE

Heliotropium arborescens | one 4- to 6-inch pot

ALTERNATES: 'Fragrant Delight' heliotrope or another 8- to 12-inch-tall, bushy plant with purple flowers, such as 'Graffiti Violet' starflower (*Pentas lanceolata*) or **LUSCIOUS GRAPE** lantana (*Lantana camara* 'Robpwpur')

3. PERSIAN SHIELD

Strobilanthes dyerianus
one 4- to 6-inch pot

ALTERNATES:
Another 18- to 24-inch-tall plant with deep purple foliage or purple flowers, such as 'Purple Knight' alternanthera (*Alternanthera dentata*), 'Osmin' basil (*Ocimum basilicum*), or 'Little One' Brazilian vervain (*Verbena bonariensis*)

4. PURPLE HEART

Setcreasea pallida one 4-inch pot

ALTERNATES: Another bushy to somewhat trailing, 6- to 8-inch-tall plant with deep purple foliage, such as **CHARMED VELVET** ('Jroxachvel') or **CHARMED WINE** ('Jroxburwi') oxalis (*Oxalis*) or 'Sweet Caroline Purple' sweet potato vine (*Ipomoea batatas*)

5. SUPERBELLS GRAPE PUNCH CALIBRACHOA

Calibrachoa 'Uscal84704' one 4-inch pot

ALTERNATES: **MINIFAMOUS COMPACT DARK BLUE** ('Kleca07129') calibrachoa or another trailing, purple-flowered plant, such as 'Fancy' fanflower (*Scaevola aemula*), **SUPERTUNIA ROYAL VELVET** petunia (*Petunia* 'Kakegawa S28'), or 'Aztec Blue Velvet' verbena (*Verbena*)

REGAL PURPLE
season by season

There's no doubt about the color theme of this container collection right from the moment you put it together, thanks to the emphatically purple leaves of purple heart, the purple-and-silver foliage of Persian shield, and the early blooms on 'Angelina Dark Purple' angelonia, 'Marine' heliotrope, and **SUPERBELLS GRAPE PUNCH** calibrachoa.

Of these five purples, Persian shield is the most cold-sensitive, so wait until nighttime temperatures are consistently above 55°F/13°F before putting the plants together in the container. Water lightly after planting.

This container offers a profusion of purple from early summer on, as all of the plants keep getting leafier and more flower-filled. The sweet scent of the 'Marine' heliotrope is an added bonus. There will probably be a few pinkish flowers on the purple heart as well.

There's not much you need to do now for your pretty-in-purple spectacle, other than regular watering (letting the top 1 to 2 inches of potting soil dry out in between) and applying a liquid fertilizer every 7 to 10 days.

TIDBITS TIPS AND TRICKS

PURPLE PLANTS FOR SHADE. This sumptuous purple planter is perfectly suited for a sunny site, but you can also enjoy it in a place that gets shade for part of the day. In fact, a spot with some shade during the hottest part of the afternoon can be ideal for the heliotrope, especially in hot-summer areas. If you want to place this planter where there's less than 6 hours of sun a day, replace the recommended blooming plants with some that are better adapted to low-light conditions, such as **SUMMER WAVE LARGE VIOLET** ('Sunrenilamu') or **PURPLE MOON** ('Dantopur') wishbone flowers (*Torenia*), **ENDLESS ILLUMINATION** browallia (*Browallia* 'Unhbr12'), 'Big Purple' or 'Purple King' achimenes (*Achimenes*), and **INFINITY LAVENDER** New Guinea impatiens (*Impatiens hawkeri* 'Vinflavimp').

During the hottest part of the summer, flower production may slow down on the 'Marine' heliotrope and **SUPERBELLS GRAPE PUNCH** calibrachoa, but the 'Angelina Dark Purple' angelonia continues to send up new bloom spikes, and the lush leaves of purple heart and Persian shield are still spectacular.

Maintain the same watering and fertilizing routine from earlier in the summer. Some time spent grooming the plants now will keep them looking their best through the rest of the summer and on into fall. Remove any dead or damaged leaves, and snip off the finished flower spikes on the angelonia and browned flower clusters on the heliotrope. If the calibrachoa isn't blooming much, clip the stems back by about a third to encourage the plant to branch out and produce new flower buds.

'Angelina Dark Purple' angelonia, 'Marine' heliotrope, and **SUPERBELLS GRAPE PUNCH** calibrachoa keep flowering well into fall, continuing to complement the lovely leaves of the purple heart and Persian shield until frost calls a halt to the growing season.

Continue watering as long as the plants are still growing. There's no need to fertilize now, though. Covering the plants with a sheet at night can help to get them through a light frost or two. Eventually, the Persian shield will start dropping its leaves, and a freeze will kill the rest of the plants; at that point, pull them out and toss them in your compost pile. (Purple heart is pretty easy to keep as a houseplant over the winter, so if you want to try to save it, take stem cuttings in early fall, or dig it out of the container before frost, plant it in a pot, and keep it on a sunny windowsill.)

PALER PURPLES. If you prefer your purples on the lighter side, replace one or more of the violet or royal purples with paler lavender or lilac tints. Instead of 'Marine' heliotrope (*Heliotropium arborescens*), for instance, consider 'Fragrant Delight', which turns a lighter purple as it ages. It's also easy to find paler purple versions of angelonias (*Angelonia*) and calibrachoas (*Calibrachoa*). Or, look for selections that have purple blooms with white stripes or white centers, or vice versa, such as 'AngelMist Purple Stripe' angelonia and **SUPERBELLS TRAILING LILAC MIST** calibrachoa (*Calibrachoa* 'Kleca08165').

Elegant WHITES

CRISP, CLEAN, AND SURE TO CATCH THE eye, white flowers with white-variegated leaves are a foolproof pairing for a striking container planting. It's an elegant combination for a formal setting and wonderful for echoing the white trim on houses, fences, or other outdoor features. Whites are also wonderful for brightening up shady corners, as well as decks, patios, and other areas where you tend to sit in the evening, as their pale tints are the last colors to disappear as darkness falls. Packed with a selection of beautiful blooms and striped and speckled leaves, this small-scale container would fit easily even on a tiny balcony or porch, or at the edge of a broad step.

FULL SUN TO PARTIAL SHADE

CONTAINER: 13" WIDE × 16" HIGH

PLANTS:

1 Variegated flax lily (*Dianella tasmanica* 'Variegata')

2 ANGELFACE WHITE angelonia (*Angelonia angustifolia* 'Anwhitim')

3 'Snowy Nutmeg' geranium (*Pelargonium fragrans*)

4 SUNPATIENS COMPACT WHITE IMPROVED impatiens (*Impatiens* 'Sakimp027')

5 Variegated wire vine (*Muehlenbeckia axillaris* 'Tricolor')

White-marked leaves are worth including in your white planting, because they do a great job completing the theme at times when flowers aren't as abundant.

THE 5-PLANT PALETTE

1. VARIEGATED FLAX LILY

Dianella tasmanica 'Variegata' | one 6-inch pot

ALTERNATES: Another 12- to 18-inch-tall plant with spiky, white-variegated foliage, such as variegated Japanese iris (*Iris ensata* 'Variegata'), variegated society garlic (*Tulbaghia violacea* 'Variegata'), or 'Sparkler' sedge (*Carex phyllocephala*)

2. ANGELFACE WHITE ANGELONIA

Angelonia angustifolia 'Anwhitim' | one 4-inch pot

ALTERNATES: 'Archangel White', 'Serenita White', or another white angelonia, or another 8- to 12-inch-tall plant with spikes or clusters of white flowers, such as 'Buddy White' globe amaranth (*Gomphrena globosa*) or 'Graffiti White' starflower (*Pentas lanceolata*)

4. SUNPATIENS COMPACT WHITE IMPROVED IMPATIENS

Impatiens 'Sakimp027' | one 4-inch pot

ALTERNATES: 'Harmony White' or another white impatiens, or another 6- to 12-inch-tall, bushy plant with white flowers, such as **SUPERTUNIA WHITE** petunia (*Petunia* 'Kakegawa S30'), 'Titan Pure White' rose periwinkle (*Catharanthus roseus*), or white heliotrope (*Heliotropium arborescens* 'Alba')

3. 'SNOWY NUTMEG' GERANIUM

Pelargonium fragrans | one 4-inch pot

ALTERNATES: Another 6- to 10-inch-tall, bushy plant with white-variegated foliage and/or white flowers, such as **FROSTY KNIGHT** sweet alyssum (*Lobularia maritima* 'Inlbupripr') or **BREATHLESS WHITE** ('Balbrewite') or **DIAMOND FROST** ('Inneuphe') spurge (*Euphorbia hypericifolia*)

5. VARIEGATED WIRE VINE

Muehlenbeckia axillaris 'Tricolor' | one 4-inch pot

ALTERNATES: Another 1- to 4-inch-tall, trailing plant with white-variegated leaves, such as variegated basket grass (*Oplismenus hirtellus* 'Variegatus'), variegated climbing fig (*Ficus pumila* 'Variegata'), or 'Anne Marie' English ivy (*Hedera helix*)

ELEGANT WHITES
season by season

The **ANGELFACE WHITE** angelonia and **SUNPATIENS COMPACT WHITE IMPROVED** impatiens will likely have a few open flowers when you find them for sale, and variegated flax lily may produce some small, starry, lavender-blue blooms in mid to late spring. But even without flowers, this container will be beautiful right from the start, thanks to the brightly patterned foliage. The spiky, green leaves of variegated flax lily are showily striped with white along the edges, making a dramatic vertical accent, while 'Snowy Nutmeg' geranium, with its scalloped, pale green leaves that are splashed with white to cream markings, forms a neat, bushy mound. Variegated wire vine, with tiny, rounded, green leaves that are speckled with white, particularly near the shoot tips, fills the space around the base of the other plants.

Wait until nighttime temperatures are at least 50°F/10°C before setting these plants outside in their container. Once they are in place, water thoroughly.

Variegated flax lily, 'Snowy Nutmeg' geranium, and variegated wire vine continue to show off their lovely leaves as the summer gets started. Flowers now join them in earnest: broad, flat-faced discs on **SUNPATIENS COMPACT WHITE IMPROVED** impatiens, spiky clusters of tubular blooms on **ANGELFACE WHITE** angelonia, and tiny, dainty blossoms on the 'Snowy Nutmeg' scented geranium. You may also see some lingering blooms on the variegated flax lily in early summer.

Water regularly when rain is lacking to keep the potting soil from drying out, and use a liquid fertilizer every 10 to 14 days. Pick the flowers off the impatiens as they start to discolor. Remove the finished flower spikes from the flax lily as well, or leave them for the chance to get berries later in the season.

TIDBITS TIPS AND TRICKS

KEEPING YOUR WHITES BRIGHT. The purity of white flowers tends to be at its peak just as the petals open and soon after. Some can keep their stainless beauty for a week or more, but others will start turning brown after just a few days, or even more quickly in strong sun or dry conditions. So, if you're planning to keep a combination featuring white flowers in a highly visible site — by your front door, for instance — plan on picking off the past-peak flowers every day or two to keep your container planting looking its very best.

A FORMULA FOR SUCCESS WITH WHITES. Pick two or three variegated leaves with different sorts of white markings (a striped one with a spotted or

MID TO LATE SUMMER

The show of flowers and foliage just keeps getting better as the plants fill out through the summer. If the variegated flax lily flowered earlier in the season, you may see blue berries forming now.

This plant-packed container will need frequent watering during the hottest part of the summer to keep new flowers coming and the leaves looking their best. Continue to use a liquid fertilizer every 10 to 14 days. Pick off the browned flowers of the impatiens, and clip off the bloom clusters of the angelonia once all of the blossoms in the spike have finished. Regularly remove any damaged or discolored leaves as well. If any of the plants are growing particularly vigorously and crowding out their companions, cut off a few of their leaves or stems to keep them in proportion to the other plants and to the container.

FALL

You'll enjoy the bright whites in this container through early fall, at least. The young shoots of the variegated wire vine will likely develop some pinkish tints again as the weather cools down, and there may still be some blue berries on the variegated flax lily.

Keep watering and grooming the plants as long as they're still growing. To extend the life of your white container, drape a sheet over it at night if light frost is predicted. Some of these plants can take a fair bit of cold, but the impatiens and scented geranium, in particular, will be damaged by below-freezing temperatures. When you're ready to dismantle the container, discard the impatiens and angelonia in your compost pile. Pot up the three variegated plants, put them in a sunny window, and enjoy them as indoor plants for the winter.

speckled one, for example), complete the grouping with a few of your favorite white flowers, and you have a container that's guaranteed to look good from spring to frost.

BRINGING IN COLOR. If pure-white blossoms appear a little too stark or glaring to you, it's easy enough to soften the effect by choosing whites that include a touch of yellow, pink, or blue. In flowers, that extra color may come as an overall tint (palest blue, for example, or a yellow-touched cream or ivory), or it may appear along with the white — in a separate yellow center, for instance, or in a pink blush along the edges. White-variegated leaves may also include other colors, such as powder blue instead of green in the nonvariegated parts, or touches of pink in the white parts.

Sparkling SILVERS

PLANTS WITH SILVERY TO GRAY FOLIAGE
are popular accents for both garden and container
combinations. Shimmering silvers hold their own with
bright whites, intense reds, hot pinks, and deep purples in
sunny sites and add twinkles of light among green leaves
in shadier spots, while cool gray-greens and gray-blues
harmonize well with pastel blooms in any place. They're
not just companions for other colors, though: silvers and
grays can also look amazing paired with each other, as
long as you include a range of leaf shapes, surface textures,
and plant habits to give them some contrast as well. This
polished silver combination shows off beautifully in a
container that has a simple shape and muted color, where
the plants can be the stars.

FULL SUN

CONTAINER: 18" LONG × 18" WIDE × 18" HIGH

PLANTS:

1 'Berggarten' culinary sage (*Salvia officinalis*)

2 'Blue Mohawk' soft rush (*Juncus inflexus*)

3 'Lacinato' kale (*Brassica oleracea* Acephala Group)

4 'Powis Castle' artemisia (*Artemisia*)

5 'Silver Falls' silver ponyfoot (*Dichondra argentea*)

Some plants, like artemisia, get their silvery look from a coating of fine hairs on their leaves. The fuzzy covering slows down the loss of water from the foliage, making these plants well adapted to hot, sunny, dry sites.

1. 'BERGGARTEN' CULINARY SAGE

Salvia officinalis | one 4- to 6-inch pot

ALTERNATES: Another mounded, 6- to 12-inch-tall plant with broad or rounded, silvery leaves, such as 'Big Ears' lamb's ears (*Stachys byzantina*), dittany of Crete (*Origanum dictamnus*), or silver sage (*Salvia argentea*)

2. 'BLUE MOHAWK' SOFT RUSH

Juncus inflexus | one 4- to 6-inch pot

ALTERNATES: 'Blue Arrows' soft rush or another upright, 12- to 18-inch-tall plant with spiky, silvery or gray-blue foliage, such as blue chalk fingers (*Senecio vitalis*) or silver spear (*Astelia chathamica*)

3. 'LACINATO' KALE

Brassica oleracea Acephala Group | one 4- to 6-inch pot

ALTERNATES: Another upright, 18- to 30-inch-tall plant with broad, silvery to silver-blue leaves, such as honey bush (*Melianthus major*) or silver shield (*Plectranthus argentatus*)

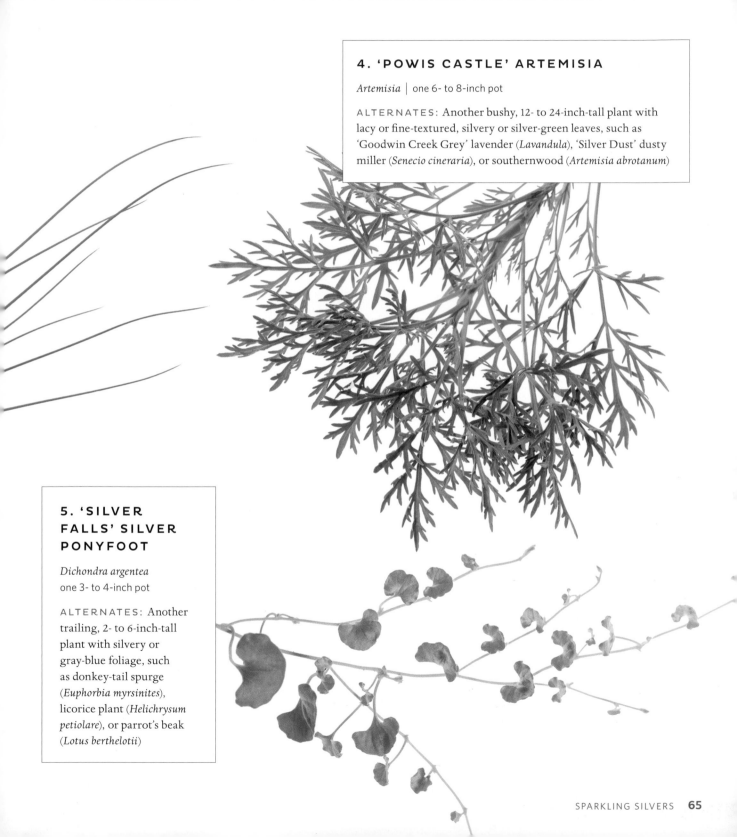

4. 'POWIS CASTLE' ARTEMISIA

Artemisia | one 6- to 8-inch pot

ALTERNATES: Another bushy, 12- to 24-inch-tall plant with lacy or fine-textured, silvery or silver-green leaves, such as 'Goodwin Creek Grey' lavender (*Lavandula*), 'Silver Dust' dusty miller (*Senecio cineraria*), or southernwood (*Artemisia abrotanum*)

5. 'SILVER FALLS' SILVER PONYFOOT

Dichondra argentea
one 3- to 4-inch pot

ALTERNATES: Another trailing, 2- to 6-inch-tall plant with silvery or gray-blue foliage, such as donkey-tail spurge (*Euphorbia myrsinites*), licorice plant (*Helichrysum petiolare*), or parrot's beak (*Lotus berthelotii*)

SPARKLING SILVERS
season by season

This container collection provides instant impact from the very first day you put it together, thanks to the fabulous foliage: bright silvery white 'Powis Castle' artemisia and 'Silver Falls' silver ponyfoot, silvery green 'Berggarten' sage, and silvery blue 'Blue Mohawk' soft rush and 'Lacinato' kale.

All five of these plants are quite tolerant of cold, as long as you don't move them suddenly from a warm greenhouse to a chilly spot outside. Once they're adapted to outside conditions, plant them in the container any time after nighttime temperatures are sure to stay above freezing. Water after planting, and use a liquid fertilizer a week or so later.

As the plants start to grow together, their various leaf shapes and textures provide as much interest as their colors. Grassy-leaved 'Blue Mohawk' soft rush is the centerpiece of the container, providing a striking contrast to the rounded 'Berggarten' sage and 'Silver Falls' silver ponyfoot, strappy 'Lacinato' kale, and lacy-leaved 'Powis Castle' artemisia.

Encourage steady growth by watering regularly (let the top inch or so of potting soil dry out in between), and use a liquid fertilizer every 10 to 14 days. If you see white butterflies fluttering around the container, or if you notice that something is chewing holes in the kale leaves, inspect the leaves for signs of of caterpillars. Pick off any caterpillars you find to immediately stop further leaf damage, and consider spraying, according to the label directions, with an organic product containing *Bacillus thuringiensis* var. *kurstaki* (*Btk*) or spinosad to prevent further damage.

TIDBITS TIPS AND TRICKS

EDIBLE SILVERS. It's easy to be entranced by the beauty of silver plants, but good looks are not all they have to offer: some of them are also edible and/or aromatic. Kales (*Brassica oleracea* Acephala Group) and cabbages (*B. oleracea* Capitata Group), for instance, often have gray-blue to gray-green leaf colors, and they can adapt easily to life in pots, making an unexpected addition to ornamental container combinations. Many herbs, too, have leaves in this color category: among them, culinary sage (*Salvia officinalis*), lavenders (*Lavandula*), lavender cotton (*Santolina chamaecyparissus*), and curry plant (*Helichrysum angustifolium*). These silvery herbs are tough enough to stand up to frequent touching, so feel free to use them in containers by a door or pathway, where you can rub their leaves to release their scent as you walk by.

You might not expect there to be much change to look forward to in a foliage-based combination like this one, but it actually continues to improve as the plants fill out and their overall shapes become apparent. 'Berggarten' sage and 'Powis Castle' artemisia are more or less mounded, though the latter is much more open, while 'Blue Mohawk' soft rush is distinctly spiky, 'Silver Falls' silver ponyfoot is gracefully cascading, and 'Lacinato' kale is almost umbrella-like in form.

Maintain the watering routine, and continue fertilizing until late summer. Also, keep watching out for pests on the kale and spraying if necessary. Every week or so, remove any dead, damaged, or discolored leaves, and clip some shoots out of the wormwood if it is starting to crowd out its companions.

This silver container continues to shine through much of the autumn, with its gently varying colors and strikingly different leaf shapes and plant forms.

Keep watering as long as the plants look good. No need to worry much about pests on the kale now; if you've kept them under control through the summer, any damage now won't seriously detract from the display. These five plants can withstand a surprising amount of cold even beyond the growing season, so you could hold off until mid or even late fall before taking apart the collection. Pull out the silver ponyfoot and kale (saving the kale leaves for cooking, if you like) and cut the thick kale stems into pieces before tossing them on your compost pile. Pot up the sage, smooth rush, and artemisia and overwinter them in a cool, bright place, such as by a sunny window in an unheated porch or attached garage.

UNUSUAL NEIGHBORS. In a garden bed, you probably wouldn't have much luck growing a drought-tolerant bright silver like 'Powis Castle' artemisia (*Artemisia*) with a moisture-loving plant like 'Blue Mohawk' soft rush (*Juncus inflexus*). You can get away with that in a container, though, because excess moisture will readily drain away (suiting the artemisia), while you can regularly add more by watering (to suit the soft rush).

BACK TO *Black*

A BLACK-BASED CONTAINER PLANTING is more than a "because you can" novelty: it's an exceptionally elegant way to display some truly distinctive and eye-catching plants. When it comes to foliage and flowers, what we call "black" is usually a shade of deep purple to burgundy red. In leaves, the color tends to be most intense in sun, but there are many outstanding black plants for less-than-full-sun sites as well. An entire collection of dark-leaved plants can be a little dull and moody, but mixing in a bit of bright green provides a quick fix, adding a touch of contrast that makes the darker parts really pop, especially in shady sites.

FULL SUN TO FULL SHADE

CONTAINER: 16" LONG × 16" WIDE × 14" HIGH

PLANTS:

1 Black mondo grass (*Ophiopogon planiscapus* 'Nigrescens')

2 'Jungle Beauty' ajuga (*Ajuga reptans*)

3 'Gotham' heuchera (*Heuchera*)

4 'Heartthrob' violet (*Viola*)

5 'Sibila' coleus (*Solenostemon scutellarioides*)

A light-colored container does a great
job showing off dark foliage and flowers,
especially in shady sites.

69

1. BLACK MONDO GRASS

Ophiopogon planiscapus 'Nigrescens' | one 3- to 4-inch pot

ALTERNATES: Another 4- to 8-inch-tall, mounded or spiky plant with dark foliage, such as 'Black Knight' echeveria (*Echeveria*) or **CHOCOLATE CHIP** ajuga (*Ajuga reptans* 'Valfredda')

2. 'JUNGLE BEAUTY' AJUGA

Ajuga reptans
one 4- to 6-inch pot

ALTERNATES: **BLACK SCALLOP** ('Binblasca') or 'Purple Brocade' ajuga or another 4- to 8-inch-tall, bushy to somewhat trailing plant with deep purple or purple-and-green leaves, such as black rose (*Aeonium arboretum* 'Zwartkop') or **CHARMED VELVET** oxalis (*Oxalis* 'Jroxachvel')

3. 'GOTHAM' HEUCHERA

Heuchera | one 4- to 6-inch pot

ALTERNATES: 'Obsidian' heuchera or another 8- to 12-inch-tall, mounded or upright plant with dark leaves, such as **BLACKBIRD** spurge (*Euphorbia* 'Nothowlee') or 'Black Velvet' or 'Midnight Twist' begonia (*Begonia*)

4. 'HEARTTHROB' VIOLET

Viola | one 3- to 4-inch pot

ALTERNATES: 'Mars' violet or another 6- to 8-inch-tall, bushy to somewhat trailing plant with black flowers or black-and-green leaves, such as 'Black Velvet' petunia (*Petunia*), 'Molly Sanderson' viola (*Viola*), or 'Black Snowflake' or 'Sugar and Spice' foamflower (*Tiarella*)

5. 'SIBILA' COLEUS

Solenostemon scutellarioides | one 3- to 4-inch pot

ALTERNATES: 'Chocolate Drop' or 'Inky Fingers' coleus or another 12- to 18-inch-tall, bushy or upright plant with near-black foliage or flowers, such as 'Chocoholic' bugbane (*Actaea*) or 'Black Star' calla lily (*Zantedeschia*)

BACK TO BLACK
season by season

SPRING

This black collection may be more of a black-and-blue theme in spring, with some purple-blue flowers if you're starting with mature plants of 'Jungle Beauty' ajuga and 'Heartthrob' violet. Most of the interest, though, comes from the lovely leaves: black-and-green on the violet and 'Sibila' coleus, and practically black on the black mondo grass, ajuga, and 'Gotham' heuchera.

The perennials in this grouping — the black mondo grass, ajuga, heuchera, and violet — are all quite cold-tolerant, so if you want to get growing as soon as possible, it's fine to put them together in the container as soon as temperatures stay above freezing. (That's assuming that the plants are already used to being outside, of course.) Wait until nighttime temperatures are at least 55°F/13°C to add the coleus to the already-planted perennials — or just wait until then to put all of the plants together. Water after planting, and supply a dose of liquid fertilizer.

EARLY TO MID SUMMER

This out-of-the-ordinary container combination just keeps getting better as the plants grow together. The dark hues, accented with touches of bright green, are a key feature, but the various leaf shapes and textures — from the glossy scallops of 'Gotham' heuchera and 'Jungle Beauty' ajuga to the spikes of black mondo grass, charming hearts of 'Heartthrob' violet, and frilly foliage of 'Sibila' coleus — add to the impact. The heuchera also contributes burgundy flower stalks topped with small, creamy white bells.

Other than watering regularly and adding liquid fertilizer every 10 to 14 days, there's not much more to do now than clip off the flowering stems of the heuchera if you don't like them, as well as any finished bloom spikes on the ajuga.

TIDBITS TIPS AND TRICKS

THE RIGHT POT. Go neutral with a pale gray or tan, or, for something really eye-catching, choose a ceramic container with a metallic-looking glaze, or even an actual silvery metal, such as brushed aluminum or galvanized steel.

A COLORFUL TOUCH. If you like black- and purple-leaved plants but don't want to go completely over to the dark side, feel free to add a touch of color to this five-plant collection by replacing one or two of the plants with white-variegated or silver foliage, or with white, bright pink, or red flowers. Or, brighten the mood with a colorful ornament or bit of decorative trellis as an accent.

MID TO LATE SUMMER

Lovely leaf colors and textures are still the stars of this darkly handsome planter later in the summer, with a few floral touches: the last of the creamy white flowers on 'Gotham' heuchera and fresh pinkish to purplish white bells on the black mondo grass.

Be sure to keep up with regular watering now if rain is lacking, and continue to fertilize every 10 to 14 days until late summer. A weekly grooming session will help the plants look their best: remove any dead or damaged foliage, and clip out any heuchera leaves or coleus stems that are crowding their companions. Cut off the finished flowering stems on the heuchera and pinch off any flower buds that form on the shoot tips of the coleus.

FALL

This black-based container collection continues to look good well into fall. The primary focus stays on the dramatic leaf colors and shapes, with the added bonus of glossy black berries on the black mondo grass and the occasional out-of-season flower on the 'Heartthrob' violet.

Continue to water regularly as long as the plants are still growing. Frost will kill the coleus, but the perennials will look good in the container into winter — even *through* the winter in mild climates. Elsewhere, it's worth moving the heuchera, ajuga, viola, and black mondo grass to your garden in early fall (in Zone 6 or 7) or potting them up and overwintering them in a cool, bright place (such as a windowsill in an unheated garage) for the winter.

SUNNING BACK THE BLACK. The five-plant grouping can get by on just a couple of hours of sun a day, but be aware that when dark-leaved plants get too much shade, they can look more greenish than black. If you notice that happening to your container combination, try moving it to a slightly brighter site. Just an extra hour or two of sun can make a big difference.

SPRING *Cheer*

CONTAINERS ARE A GIFT TO WINTER-WEARY gardeners everywhere, providing the perfect place to show off some beautiful spring blooms well before it's time to start planting in beds and borders. Brighten your life with a combination of rich, vivid colors, or celebrate the vernal season with a palette of pretty pastel blooms. This flower-filled oval basket planter showcases a collection of early-blooming annuals and perennials in cheery hues of yellow, pink, orange, and green that are sure to bring a smile to your face.

FULL SUN TO PARTIAL SHADE

CONTAINER: 18" LONG × 14" WIDE × 8" HIGH

PLANTS:

1 FLIRTATION ORANGE twinspur (*Diascia* 'Dal Oran')

2 'Sorbet Yellow XP' viola (*Viola cornuta*)

3 'Armada Rose' sea thrift (*Armeria maritima*)

4 'Frizzle Sizzle Mix' pansy (*Viola × wittrockiana*)

5 'Wonderland Purple' sweet alyssum (*Lobularia maritima*)

If late spring frosts are common in your area, consider using a lightweight container instead, so it will be easier to move if the forecast predicts freezing temperatures.

THE 5-PLANT PALETTE

1. FLIRTATION ORANGE TWINSPUR

Diascia 'Dal Oran' | one 4-inch pot

ALTERNATES: 'Sundiascia Upright Orange' or 'Romeo Orange' twinspur, or another 8- to 14-inch-tall, bushy, early-blooming plant with orange flowers, such as **ANGELART ORANGE** nemesia (*Nemesia strumosa* 'Kirine-15') or 'Citrona Orange' Siberian wallflower (*Erysimum* × *allionii*)

2. 'SORBET YELLOW XP' VIOLA

Viola cornuta | three 2- or 3-inch-tall plants

ALTERNATES: Another bright-flowered viola, such as 'Penny Yellow' (pure yellow) or 'Sorbet Sunny Royale' (purple-and-ycllow), or another 4- to 6-inch-tall, early-blooming plant, such as a yellow-flowered primrose (*Primula*)

3. 'ARMADA ROSE' SEA THRIFT

Armeria maritima | two 3- to 4-inch pots

ALTERNATES: Another compact sea thrift, such as 'Bloodstone' or 'Nifty Thrifty' (with cream-striped leaves), or another 3- to 6-inch-tall, tufted or trailing plant with rich green leaves, such as dwarf mondo grass (*Ophiopogon japonicus* 'Nana') or lesser periwinkle (*Vinca minor*)

4. 'FRIZZLE SIZZLE MIX' PANSY

Viola × wittrockiana
two 2- or 3-inch-tall plants

ALTERNATES: Another violet- or blue-flowered pansy, such as 'Crown Purple' or 'Majestic Giants II Purple with Blotch', or another 4- to 6-inch-tall, early-blooming plant with purple or blue flowers, such as 'Dixie Chip' ajuga (*Ajuga reptans*)

5. 'WONDERLAND PURPLE' SWEET ALYSSUM

Lobularia maritima | one 6-cell pack

ALTERNATES: Another purple-flowered sweet alyssum, such as 'Royal Carpet', or another 3- to 6-inch-tall, bushy, early-blooming plant with purple or blue flowers, such as blue lobelia (*Lobelia erinus*)

SPRING

The bright orange blooms of **FLIRTATION ORANGE** twinspur and the sunny yellow flowers of 'Sorbet Yellow XP' viola are the first to catch your eye in this container. As you get a bit closer, you'll appreciate the frilly blue-purples of the 'Frizzle Sizzle Mix' pansies and the dainty, deep purple blossoms of 'Wonderland Purple' sweet alyssum, too. 'Armada Rose' sea thrift starts the season as dense, rich green, grasslike tufts, accented with slender stems topped by ball-shaped clusters of pink blooms in mid to late spring.

Buy twinspur, viola, pansy, and sweet alyssum plants that are already in bloom, and sea thrift plants that are already starting to produce buds, so you can enjoy your spring container right from the start. Gradually harden off the plants over a week or so. Water right after planting, and again as needed to keep the potting soil evenly moist (but not soggy). Apply a liquid fertilizer every 7 to 10 days.

EARLY TO MID SUMMER

Though spring may be over, this container will continue to look charming through early summer, at least, as all five plants are in peak bloom.

Keep up with regular watering and fertilizing now. Clip off the flowers of the sea thrift close to the base of the stems, and pinch off the dead pansy and viola flowers to keep the planter looking its best.

Around midsummer, cut all the plants back by half to encourage bushy regrowth and rebloom. In hot-summer areas, consider moving the container to a slightly shadier spot (with morning sun and afternoon shade, or light all-day shade) for this part of the season.

TIDBITS TIPS AND TRICKS

A SPRING BASKET. If frosts still threaten when you're ready to get your potted garden started, place the finished planter in a sheltered spot and cover it with an overturned box or large pot at night. Or, choose a container that's light enough to bring inside on chilly nights. A wicker basket with a sturdy handle, such as an old Easter basket, makes a whimsical option for a collection of showy spring bloomers.

ROOM FOR BULBS. Early bulbs are a sure sign of spring, but it can be tricky to coordinate them for container plantings, because they need to be planted months before it's time to plan your spring combination. Plus, they really don't add much to the display before and after their relatively brief bloom season. They're so charming, though, that it's worth going to a little extra effort to enjoy them in an early-season container. Buy a

By midsummer, the 'Armada Rose' sea thrift has finished flowering, but its grassy green foliage looks good through the rest of the growing season. The 'Sorbet Yellow XP' viola, 'Frizzle Sizzle Mix' pansies, and 'Wonderland Purple' sweet alyssum tend to get a bit tired-looking and produce fewer flowers during the hottest part of the summer, but **FLIRTATION ORANGE** twinspur will continue to flower, so the container can still have some interest now.

Keep watering, and use a liquid fertilizer every 10 to 14 days.

If you kept your spring container going through the summer, you can enjoy a second spectacle as cooler temperatures return in autumn — not as splendid as in spring, perhaps, but still worth trying.

If any of the plants fizzled out during the hottest part of the summer and left gaps in the container, buy a new pack of violas or pansies to fill their places. Continue to water the container as long as the plants look good. As the growing season winds down, transplant the sea thrift to your garden (it should be hardy as far north as Zone 3). If the viola and pansy plants still look good, you could move them to the garden also; they may overwinter and bloom more in spring. Or, discard them on your compost pile with the nemesia and sweet alyssum.

few small pots of already-started bulbs for sale at your local greenhouse or garden center, sink them into your chosen planter (leaving them in their pots), and tuck in the other spring bloomers around them. Once the bulbs are done blooming, lift them out — pots and all — and transplant them to your garden. Tuck a few more flowering plants into the spaces left in your container display, or fill those holes with a bit of potting soil and let the remaining plants cover the space.

POTTING UP EXTRAS. Pansies and violas (*Viola*) are usually sold in packs of four or six plants, so what do you do with the leftovers after you plant your spring container? Pot them up individually for spots of color in other sites, or plant the extras in a nearby flower bed to extend your spring container display into your yard.

All-Summer COLOR

WITH SO MANY WONDERFUL SUMMER-flowering plants to choose from, the hardest part of creating a gorgeous summer display is narrowing down your choices to just five. It helps if you select one or two — or a few — favorite colors, then pick one or more bushy, upright, and trailing plants from each. A pot or planter based on flowers and foliage with vivid colors is especially good for a sun-drenched site, such as a deck or poolside, where the intense light can bleach out paler petals. The bounty of brilliant pinks, purples, and yellows in this hunter green planter is sure to brighten your life all summer long.

FULL SUN TO LIGHT SHADE

CONTAINER: 30" LONG × 18" WIDE × 18" HIGH

PLANTS:

1 CARITA PURPLE 09 angelonia (*Angelonia angustifolia* 'Car Purr09')

2 'Electric Lime' coleus (*Solenostemon scutellarioides*)

3 Golden creeping Jenny (*Lysimachia nummularia* 'Aurea')

4 'Golden Edge' golden dewdrop (*Duranta erecta*)

5 'Profusion Double Cherry' zinnia (*Zinnia*)

Plant-packed containers like this one look good quickly, but they can get overcrowded by mid to late summer, and then flower production starts to suffer. So, don't be afraid to get in there with your pruning shears or garden scissors every week or two.

1. CARITA PURPLE 09 ANGELONIA

Angelonia angustifolia 'Car Purr09' | two 3- to 4-inch pots

ALTERNATES: 'Serena Purple' or **ANGELFACE BLUE** ('Anblauzwei') angelonia, or another 18- to 24-inch-tall, upright annual with rich purple flowers, such as 'Evolution Violet' mealy-cup sage (*Salvia farinacea*) or heliotrope (*Heliotropium arborescens*)

2. 'ELECTRIC LIME' COLEUS

Solenostemon scutellarioides one 3- to 4-inch pot

ALTERNATES: 'Limon Blush' or another yellow, orangey, or multicolored, sun-tolerant coleus, or another 12- to 18-inch-tall, bushy plant with bright yellow foliage, such as 'Limelight' four-o'clock (*Mirabilis jalapa*)

3. GOLDEN CREEPING JENNY

Lysimachia nummularia 'Aurea' | one 3- to 4-inch pot

ALTERNATES: Another 3- to 6-inch-tall, low-mounded to trailing plant with yellow leaves, such as golden oregano (*Origanum vulgare* 'Aureum') or 'Angelina' sedum (*Sedum rupestre*)

4. 'GOLDEN EDGE' GOLDEN DEWDROP

Duranta erecta
one 3- to 4-inch pot

ALTERNATES:
Another 18- to 30-inch-
tall, bushy plant with
bright yellow or yellow-
and-green leaves, such
as 'Mickie' rock rose
(*Cistus × hybridus*) or
SUNSHINE BLUE blue-
beard (*Caryopteris incana*
'Jason')

5. 'PROFUSION DOUBLE CHERRY' ZINNIA

Zinnia | one 3- to 4-inch pot

ALTERNATES: 'Dreamland Rose', 'Zahara Double Cherry',
or another compact, bright pink zinnia, or another 10- to
14-inch-tall, bushy plant with bright pink flowers, such as
'Cora Cascade Cherry' rose periwinkle (*Catharanthus roseus*)

ALL-SUMMER COLOR

season by season

SPRING

This collection provides a punch of color right from planting time, thanks to the bright yellow in the leaves of the 'Electric Lime' coleus, golden creeping Jenny, and 'Golden Edge' golden dewdrop.

Buy the plants as you find them and keep them in a warm, bright spot. Wait until all danger of frost has passed and night temperatures are consistently above 55°F/13°C or so before planting them outside in your container. (It can be tempting to get an earlier start, but if a sudden cold snap stunts the plants, it may set back the peak summer display by several weeks.)

EARLY TO MID SUMMER

The cheery yellow foliage of the 'Electric Lime' coleus, golden creeping Jenny, and 'Golden Edge' golden dewdrop is still the main source of color in early summer, but it's quickly joined by the first, daisy-form flowers of the 'Profusion Double Cherry' zinnia, which open in an intense shade of near-red. The CARITA PURPLE 09 angelonia joins in now, too, with spikes of simple but showy, rich purple blooms.

If the weather didn't cooperate in late spring, you can still start your container in early summer. The plants will thrive in the warmer conditions and fill in quickly. Water regularly to support the speedy growth; other than that, this collection needs little maintenance right now.

TIDBITS TIPS AND TRICKS

EASY ON THE BACK. A large planter, like this one, can be extremely heavy to move once it's filled with potting soil. Consider buying two or three smaller plastic pots of the same depth that can fit snugly inside, and plant into them instead. If you want to change the planter when the season changes, simply pull out those pots and replace them with others that you planted a few weeks earlier, and your container display won't miss a beat.

MANAGING COLEUS. Coleus (*Solenostemon scutellarioides*) is a classic choice for bringing foliage color to shady spots, and now there are sun-tolerant types that are just right for bright sites. They also start producing spikes of bluish white flowers at the stem tips in summer, but the blossoms aren't as attractive as the leaves, so it's best to clip them

July and August are the peak season for this planter, just in time for summertime celebrations and outdoor entertaining. The bushy mound of the 'Profusion Double Cherry' is practically smothered with fully opened, hot pink blooms, and the dense spikes of the **CARITA PURPLE 09** angelonia are filled with purple flowers. The lush leaves of 'Electric Lime' coleus, golden creeping Jenny, and 'Golden Edge' golden dewdrop continue their brilliant yellow display.

To keep the zinnia at peak prettiness, pinch or clip off the blooms as soon as they begin to fade to make room for the fresh flowers. The individual angelonia blossoms drop off on their own, but new buds keep opening as the spikes grow upward. Once all of the buds on a spike have opened, clip off the spent spike just above the leafy part of the stem. Prune out any overly long stems to keep the whole container looking balanced.

These prolific plants keep the color coming well into fall, until cold weather calls a halt to the display, so you can easily get a month or more of bonus beauty from this summer-themed collection.

Keep fertilizing into early fall, and continue to water regularly. Take cuttings of the coleus and golden dewdrop in early fall, if you want to try to keep them indoors through the winter. Once the container has been nipped by frost, pull out the angelonia, coleus, and zinnia and toss them in your compost pile. The golden dewdrop stems are thorny and tend to be tough, so you may want to clip them off before composting its roots. Golden creeping Jenny is perennial in Zones 3 to 9, so you can plant it in the ground or transplant it into a pot and give it a cool, bright spot for the winter.

off as they form; that will also encourage the plants to be bushier. Or, save yourself that task by choosing cutting-grown (also known as vegetatively propagated) coleus plants, which tend to be much slower to form flowers and so need far less pinching than less-expensive seed-grown types.

AUTUMN'S
Brilliance

WHY BE SATISFIED WITH CONTAINERS that fizzle out by the end of the summer? Mixing up your plant choices a bit can give you a combination that looks better and better as the growing season goes on, providing a wealth of changing colors and interesting elements for a splendid late-season spectacle. There are three key things to think about for fabulous fall containers: showy seed heads, intriguing fruits, and bright fall foliage. Paired with long-blooming and late-blooming flowers and red, purple, or yellow leaves, as in this burgundy-colored planter, these bonus features bring the feeling of autumn abundance to even a small space.

FULL SUN TO LIGHT SHADE

CONTAINER: 14" LONG × 14" WIDE × 24" HIGH

PLANTS:

1 'Autumnale' fuchsia (*Fuchsia*)

2 'Fireworks' fountain grass (*Pennisetum setaceum*)

3 'My Love' Chinese plumbago (*Ceratostigma willmottianum*)

4 'Sangria' ornamental pepper (*Capsicum annuum*)

5 'Tor' birchleaf spirea (*Spiraea betulifolia*)

Ornamental peppers are an excellent choice for adding summer and fall color to sunny containers. The 'Sangria' variety produces mild fruits safe for youngsters.

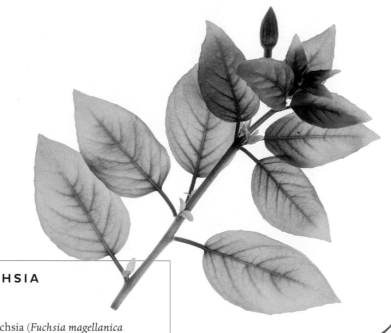

1. 'AUTUMNALE' FUCHSIA

Fuchsia | one 3- to 4-inch pot

ALTERNATES: Golden hardy fuchsia (*Fuchsia magellanica* 'Aurea') or another 3- to 6-inch-tall, bushy or trailing plant with yellow or yellow-variegated leaves, such as or 'Walkabout Sunset' dense-flowered loosestrife (*Lysimachia congestiflora*)

2.'FIREWORKS' FOUNTAIN GRASS

Pennisetum setaceum one 4- to 6-inch pot

ALTERNATES: Purple fountain grass (*Pennisetum setaceum* 'Rubrum') or another 2- to 3-foot-tall, upright to arching ornamental grass with purple or reddish leaves, such as 'Cheyenne Sky' switch grass (*Panicum virgatum*) or 'Jester' millet (*Pennisetum glaucum*)

3. 'MY LOVE' CHINESE PLUMBAGO

Ceratostigma willmottianum | one 3- to 4-inch pot

ALTERNATES: Leadwort (*Ceratostigma plumbaginoides*) or another 4- to 8-inch-tall, bushy or trailing plant with autumn flowers and/or fall foliage color, such as 'Sentimental Blue' balloon flower (*Platycodon grandiflorus*)

4. 'SANGRIA' ORNAMENTAL PEPPER

Capsicum annuum
one 3- to 4-inch pot

ALTERNATES:
Another 6- to 10-inch-tall ornamental pepper, such as 'Chilly Chili' or 'Masquerade'

5. 'TOR' BIRCHLEAF SPIREA

Spiraea betulifolia
one 6- to 8-inch pot

ALTERNATES:
Another 8- to 16-inch-tall, deciduous shrub or tree with colorful fall foliage, such as 'Firepower' or 'Harbour Dwarf' heavenly bamboo (*Nandina domestica*), a small Japanese maple (*Acer palmatum*), or **TIGER EYES** sumac (*Rhus typhina* 'Bailtiger')

AUTUMN'S BRILLIANCE
season by season

Even a pot planned for fall interest can look great all through the growing season if you combine plants with eye-catching foliage. This grouping gives you red-tinged to orangey yellow colors from the 'Autumnale' fuchsia, bright yellow from the 'My Love' Chinese plumbago, rich reddish pink from the 'Fireworks' fountain grass, and blue-green from the 'Tor' birchleaf spirea right from the start, and just gets better as the plants mature. 'Tor' birchleaf spirea also contributes small clusters of tiny white flowers in late spring.

Buy the plants as you find them, but keep those that are already actively growing in a warm, sheltered spot. Wait until nighttime temperatures are at least 55°F/13°C before planting so the fountain grass and pepper don't get stunted by the cold. Or, pot up the other plants once the danger of frost has passed and tuck pots of pansies (*Viola*) or other early bloomers in the empty spaces until you can replace them with the fountain grass and pepper.

Leaf colors and textures provide the main interest to this collection at this time, possibly with some early blooms on the fuchsia.

If you didn't get your fall container planted in late spring, you can do it in early or even mid summer and still get a spectacular autumn display. Snip the flower heads off the birchleaf spirea once the blooms fade, and through the summer trim any of its stems that are crowding the other plants. Water regularly to keep the potting soil from drying out.

TIDBITS TIPS AND TRICKS

SEASONAL DISTINCTIONS. If you like your containers to have a more distinctive change from summer to autumn, use a summer-lovely annual, such as a compact zinnia, as one of the bushy or trailing plants, and then replace it with something fresh for fall. Consider a small potted mum (*Chrysanthemum*) to emphasize the autumn theme, or choose pansies (*Viola* × *wittrockiana*) or pot marigolds (*Calendula officinalis*) for a splash of cool-season color.

TREES AND SHRUBS WITH EARLY COLOR. 'Tor' birchleaf spirea (*Spiraea betulifolia*) is one of my favorite shrubs for fall color, but it may not develop its best colors until late October. If you usually have your first frost earlier than that, consider a tree or shrub that tends to color up sooner, such as a small maple (*Acer*) or dwarf heavenly

MID TO LATE SUMMER

The colorful foliage is joined by a variety of flowers in mid to late summer, including purple-and-red pendants on the fuchsia, brilliant blue blossoms on the Chinese plumbago, and fluffy pink spikes on the fountain grass. The ornamental pepper has tiny white flowers, too, but they're much less noticeable than the slender, upward-pointing fruits they produce — usually in shades of orange to purple at this point in the season.

The leaves of the fuchsia and Chinese plumbago may get a little crispy in intense summer sun, especially if the potting soil dries out, so water frequently, especially during hot, dry weather. Pinch or snip off any damaged leaves, if desired, to keep the pot looking its best. Use a liquid fertilizer to support the burst of growth during this time.

FALL

Abundance is the key feature of this autumncentric container: lush leaves, beautiful blooms, fabulous fruits, and lots of bright colors all around. The fuchsia and Chinese plumbago are at peak bloom now; the fountain grass is full of tall, arching, tan tails; and the pepper is loaded with red and purple fruits. A red blush becomes prominent on the yellow leaves of the fuchsia as the weather cools, and 'Tor' birchleaf spirea eventually contributes shades of purple, red, orange, and yellow.

Continue watering regularly. Covering the plants with a sheet on nights when light frosts are predicted can help extend the display well into fall. Freezing temperatures will call an end to the peak display. Transplant the Chinese plumbago and birchleaf spirea to your garden, if you wish. Chinese plumbago is hardy in Zones 6 to 9, and birchleaf spirea is hardy in Zones 3 to 8. It's easiest to treat the other plants as annuals and compost them at the end of the growing season.

bamboo (*Nandina*). Use it in the container for a year or two and then transplant it to your garden when it gets too big.

FALL-THEMED ACCESSORIES. Want a quick way to jazz up your fall container for a special autumn event? Tuck some tiny pumpkins or gourds among the plants and place a few larger ones around the base of the pot. To add excitement up high, push some cut branches of berries or fall-colored leaves into the center or back of the container as a vertical accent.

WINTER
Wonders

THE END OF THE GROWING SEASON
doesn't have to mean the end of enjoying beautiful
containers. Instead of depending on flowers for color,
focus on plants that have wonderful winter features,
such as bright stems or evergreen leaves. You'll still
get to enjoy it in other seasons, as the plants produce
lush new leaves in spring and summer and go in and
out of bloom in summer and fall. All of the plants
in this grouping are normally hardy to at least Zone
5, but in a container, this collection is best suited to
Zone 7 and areas south, or perhaps Zone 6 in a very
sheltered spot.

FULL SUN TO PARTIAL SHADE

CONTAINER: 18" LONG × 18" WIDE × 18" HIGH

PLANTS:

1 ARCTIC FIRE red-osier dogwood (*Cornus sericea* 'Farrow')

2 'Danica' eastern arborvitae (*Thuja occidentalis*)

3 'Gold Child' English ivy (*Hedera helix*)

4 'Melting Fire' heuchera (*Heuchera*)

5 Variegated lilyturf (*Liriope muscari* 'Variegata')

For winter containers, choose a material that can hold up to freezing temperatures without cracking or crumbling, such as wood or resin.

THE 5-PLANT PALETTE

1. ARCTIC FIRE RED-OSIER DOGWOOD

Cornus sericea 'Farrow' | one 6- to 8-inch pot

ALTERNATES: Another 18- to 24-inch-tall, shrubby dogwood
with colorful stems, such as *Cornus sericea* 'Kelseyi' or *C. alba*
'Siberian Pearls' (both red), or *C. sericea* 'Bud's Yellow'

2. 'DANICA' EASTERN ARBORVITAE

Thuja occidentalis
one 6- to 8-inch pot

ALTERNATES:
Another 8- to 12-inch-
tall, mounded or
spreading conifer with
green or blue foliage,
such as dwarf Hinoki
cypress (*Chamaecyparis
obtusa* 'Nana') or dwarf
moss falsecypress
(*C. pisifera* 'Squarrosa
Minima')

3. 'GOLD CHILD' ENGLISH IVY

Hedera helix | one 4- to 6-inch pot

ALTERNATES: Another English ivy that is yellow or
yellow-variegated, such as 'Buttercup' or 'Yellow Ripple', or
solid green, such as 'Duckfoot' or 'Needlepoint', or another
3- to 6-inch-tall, trailing evergreen, such as 'Illumination' lesser
periwinkle (*Vinca minor*)

4. 'MELTING FIRE' HEUCHERA

Heuchera │ one 6- to 8-inch pot

ALTERNATES: Another 6- to 12-inch-tall (in leaf) heuchera, such as 'Blackout' or 'Obsidian' for purple foliage or 'Caramel' or 'Southern Comfort' if you'd prefer coppery orange

5. VARIEGATED LILYTURF

Liriope muscari 'Variegata' │ one 6- to 8-inch pot

ALTERNATES: 'Silvery Sunproof' or MARC ANTHONY ('Marant') lilyturf for variegated foliage or 'Big Blue' or EMERALD GODDESS ('Love Potion No. 13') lilyturf for solid green leaves, or another 6- to 12-inch-tall, spiky to arching evergreen perennial with slender leaves, such as 'Evergold' Japanese sedge (*Carex oshimensis*)

WINTER WONDERS
season by season

SPRING

While this container is meant for winter interest, it's colorful in spring, too, with green and yellow from the 'Gold Child' English ivy and variegated lilyturf, bronzy green from the 'Danica' eastern arborvitae, and deep red from the stems of **ARCTIC FIRE** red-osier dogwood and new leaves of 'Melting Fire' heuchera.

When you're starting this container from scratch, it's fine to put the plants together as soon as you get them, as long as they're already used to outdoor temperatures. (If they've been growing in a greenhouse, gradually expose them to outdoor conditions over a period of a week or so, and be prepared to cover them at night if frost is predicted.) In following years, simply trim off any winter-damaged leaves and shoots in early spring. You may also want to give the variegated lilyturf a complete trim — back to about 2 inches tall — around that time to make room for the fresh, new growth.

EARLY TO MID SUMMER

The basic colors of this container collection — green, yellow, and deep red — stay the same all year, but they're especially vibrant now, with all of the new leafy growth. Don't be surprised to see that the new shoots on the red-osier dogwood are green, not red; they'll color up later in the year. 'Melting Fire' heuchera usually starts sending up its bloom stems in early summer. Individually, the tiny white flowers aren't especially showy, but they're so abundant that they add a pretty cloud of bloom by midsummer.

Water regularly to keep the soil evenly moist, which will encourage quick, lush growth. A dose or two of liquid fertilizer can also help.

TIDBITS TIPS AND TRICKS

THE RIGHT HARDINESS ZONE. Containers offer much more challenging conditions than in-ground gardens for plants in winter, because the raised roots are much more exposed to cold and to frequent freezing and thawing. So when you're choosing perennials and shrubs for winter containers, look for those that are hardy to at *least* one hardiness zone colder than yours; two or more zones is even better. If you're in Zone 7, for instance, it's best to choose plants that are winter-hardy to at least Zone 5.

PREVENTING WATER LOSS. Evergreen perennials and shrubs can be susceptible to browning in winter, especially if they're exposed to drying winds, if the weather stays below freezing for longer periods, or if you forget to water the container occasionally. Keeping your winter container in a site that's sheltered from wind can help

Lovely leaves continue to be the key feature of this container later in the summer, with the addition of a pop of color from the purple-blue bloom spikes on the variegated lilyturf. The flowers of 'Melting Fire' heuchera start slowing down in late summer, but unlike many heucheras, its bloom stalks continue to look pretty good even when the blossoms drop.

Keep watering, especially during hot, dry spells, and treat the plants to another dose or two of liquid fertilizer in midsummer. If you wish, cut off the finished flower spikes of the heuchera close to the base of the plant to encourage new spikes. Check the shoot tips of the dogwood, and crush any aphids you see. If you see holes in the dogwood leaves, check for the black-and-white or powdery white, caterpillar-like larvae of sawflies on the underside of the leaves. Pick them off and crush them or drop them into soapy water.

This five-plant grouping keeps looking lush and leafy into early fall, with the addition of the variegated lilyturf flowers often continuing to mid fall. The return of cool temperatures also brings out a burgundy blush on the ARCTIC FIRE red-osier dogwood foliage. After its leaves drop, the current year's growth darkens to the red winter color. It's normal for the bright green foliage of 'Danica' eastern arborvitae to take on a bronzy cast in winter.

No need to fertilize now, but keep watering during dry spells, even in winter. Trim off the flower stems of the variegated lilyturf once the flowers drop. Also clip off any remaining bloom stalks on the 'Melting Fire' heuchera. Through the winter, occasionally trim off any damaged leaves to keep the container looking its best.

to prevent damage. To minimize water loss through the leaves, treat them with an antidessicant spray, such as Wilt-Pruf, in mid to late fall.

PLANTS FOR COLDER CONDITIONS. What about winter containers for cold climates? Replace some or all of the live plants with cut stems and greens instead. Gather evergreens, colorful stems, and berry-filled branches from your yard, or buy them in late fall from a place that sells fresh materials for holiday decorating. Stick in some interesting seed heads (spritz them with spray paint first to give them a dash of color, if you wish), or skewer oranges, apples, and other fruits on sticks and insert them as accents.

YEAR-ROUND
Interest

CONTAINERS IN HIGH-VISIBILITY SPOTS, such as by your front door or next to a frequently used walkway, need to be lush and colorful for as long as possible. First, look to the leaves for features such as variegation, interesting leaf shapes and textures, and evergreen foliage. Then, try to find plants with at least one other striking seasonal feature, such as contrasting new shoots, beautiful blooms, or autumn color changes. Based on creams, greens, and bronzy colors, this particular multiseason combination is best suited for containers in Zone 7 and south.

FULL SUN TO LIGHT SHADE

CONTAINER: 18" LONG × 18" WIDE × 18" HIGH

PLANTS:

1 'Alaska' nasturtium (*Tropaeolum majus*)

2 'Circus' heuchera (*Heuchera*)

3 'Goshiki' false holly (*Osmanthus heterophyllus*)

4 'Red Rooster' leatherleaf sedge (*Carex buchananii*)

5 'Wojo's Jem' greater periwinkle (*Vinca major*)

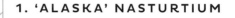

1. 'ALASKA' NASTURTIUM

Tropaeolum majus │ two 3- to 4-inch pots

ALTERNATES: Another 4- to 6-inch-tall, trailing plant with cream-variegated or chartreuse foliage, such as 'Limelight' licorice plant (*Helichrysum petiolare*), or with cream or soft yellow flowers, such as **SUPERBELLS LEMON CHIFFON** calibrachoa (*Calibrachoa* 'Uscali4021') or 'Lanai Lime Green' verbena (*Verbena*)

2. 'CIRCUS' HEUCHERA

Heuchera
one 6- to 8-inch pot

ALTERNATES: Another 6- to 12-inch-tall (in leaf) heuchera with cream-to-yellow or peach-colored foliage, such as 'Caramel', 'Delta Dawn', 'Miracle', or 'Tiramisu' heuchera

3. 'GOSHIKI' FALSE HOLLY

Osmanthus heterophyllus
one 6- to 8-inch pot

ALTERNATES: Another 14- to 24-inch-tall evergreen shrub with variegated leaves, such as such as 'Golden Triumph' or **WEDDING RING** ('Eseles') littleleaf boxwood (*Buxus microphylla*); silver-variegated English holly (*Ilex aquifolium* 'Argentea-Marginata'); or variegated pittosporum (*Pittosporum tobira* 'Variegata')

4. 'RED ROOSTER' LEATHERLEAF SEDGE

Carex buchananii | one 6- to 8-inch pot

ALTERNATES: A different bronze-leaved sedge, such as 'Bronze' New Zealand hair sedge (*Carex comans*) or *C. flagellifera* 'Toffee Twist', or another 8- to 18-inch-tall, spiky plant with bronzy to orangey leaves, such as New Zealand iris (*Libertia peregrinans*)

5. 'WOJO'S JEM' GREATER PERIWINKLE

Vinca major | one 3- to 4-inch pot

ALTERNATES: Variegated greater periwinkle ('Variegata') or 'Illumination', 'Moonlit', or 'Ralph Shugert' lesser periwinkle (*V. minor*), or another 3- to 6-inch-tall, trailing evergreen with yellow- to cream-variegated leaves, such as 'Golden Ingot' English ivy (*Hedera helix*)

YEAR-ROUND INTEREST
season by season

This multiseason container looks good right from the start, thanks to the fantastic foliage plants. 'Wojo's Jem' greater periwinkle has bright green leaves with creamy white centers, which echo the creamy white speckling in the 'Goshiki' false holly foliage. The new leaves of 'Circus' heuchera are generally a coppery pink now, picking up the colors of the 'Red Rooster' leatherleaf sedge as well as the newest shoots of the false holly.

You can plant the heuchera, false holly, leatherleaf sedge, and greater periwinkle as soon as the weather's warm enough for you to work outside comfortably (if the plants have been hardened off, of course). In following years, this is the time to snip off any damaged leaves and shoots, trim the false holly and greater periwinkle so they look tidy and well shaped, and divide the heuchera and leatherleaf sedge if needed. In late spring, tuck in a few seeds or small plants of 'Alaska' nasturtium. Water occasionally to keep the potting soil evenly moist.

'Wojo's Jem' greater periwinkle is usually about done blooming now, but its variegated foliage still looks fresh and bright, as does that of the 'Alaska' nasturtium and 'Goshiki' false holly. 'Goshiki' is so heavily speckled now that once the new leaves lose their coppery tint, they can appear almost solid cream. 'Circus' heuchera is especially colorful around this time, with creamy green older leaves, chartreuse new leaves that are veined with red, and airy sprays of reddish pink flowers. The newer leaves of 'Red Rooster' leatherleaf sedge often still have a coppery pink tint, while the older leaves are fully bronze.

There's not much to do now, other than watering regularly and supplying a liquid fertilizer every few weeks to encourage lush growth.

TIDBITS TIPS AND TRICKS

CONTAINER FOR THE COLD. Winter is the toughest time of year to keep containers of live plants looking good, particularly north of Zone 7. To increase your chance of success, choose a freeze-proof container with sides that are at least 1 inch thick. That will help to protect the roots from damage due to rapid freezing and thawing in winter. (It will insulate them from intense summer heat, too.) If you want to use a container with thinner sides, consider lining it with bubble wrap or sheets of Styrofoam before adding the potting soil or slipping in a plastic "liner" pot. Placing your container in a site that's well protected from drying winter winds can also be a huge help in keeping evergreen plants looking good during the colder months.

MID TO LATE SUMMER

'Circus' heuchera finishes up flowering by late summer, and its leaves usually lose their reddish veining in hot weather, so the plant is mostly a lush mound of broad, yellow-green to creamy green leaves now. 'Wojo's Jem' greater periwinkle, 'Goshiki' false holly, and 'Alaska' nasturtium continue to be lovely cream-and-green foliage accents in late summer, with the addition of red, orange, gold, or yellow flowers on the nasturtium.

When the heuchera is finished flowering, clip off the bloom stems close to the base of the plant. Keep watering regularly, especially during hot, dry spells. Add another dose or two of liquid fertilizer, but stop by late summer so your plants can start getting ready for the colder weather.

FALL AND WINTER

The return of cool weather tends to bring back the reddish veining on the 'Circus' heuchera leaves; by midwinter, they're typically a silvery light green to bronzy green. Cold may also bring out a bit of an orangey pink blush on some of the 'Wojo's Jem' leaves, and sometimes a few late flowers as well. The periwinkle leaves, along with the speckled 'Goshiki' false holly and the bronzy 'Red Rooster' leatherleaf sedge, hold their colors through the winter. 'Alaska' nasturtium often looks its best in fall, with an abundance of variegated leaves and lots of flowers, and continues until frost.

Pull out the nasturtiums once they get zapped by below-freezing temperatures, and add some mulch to cover the bare potting soil. Other than watering occasionally so the soil doesn't dry out completely, and spraying once or twice with Wilt-Pruf or another antidessicant to protect the leaves from drying winds, this four-season container needs little attention in fall and winter.

CHANGING INTERESTS. Keeping the same container planting all year long doesn't mean that you're stuck with the same look season after season. For a bit of extra spring color, tuck in a small pot or two of forced bulbs, or a few small plants of sweet alyssum (*Lobularia maritima*), blue lobelia (*Lobelia erinus*), or another small cool-season annual in early to mid spring. Pull them out in summer, once the perennials have filled in; and add an ornament or a bit of decorative trellising. Fall fruits and veggies make fun autumn accents, while cut greens or berried branches add zip for winter.

MADE *for* SHADE

A SHADY DECK, PORCH, OR PATIO IS A wonderful place to relax on a hot summer day; it's also a great opportunity to indulge in some lush, colorful containers of shade-loving plants. Classic annuals for shady sites, like impatiens (*Impatiens*) and begonias (*Begonia*), come in many interesting options, but these traditional favorites are just the beginning. You can also find some stunning shady characters in the perennials section at your favorite garden center, and among displays of tropicals and houseplants. This cubic, glazed container includes a variety of hardy and tender plants with colorful leaves and flowers for a stunning show all through the growing season.

PARTIAL TO FULL SHADE

CONTAINER: 16" LONG × 16" WIDE × 16" HIGH

PLANTS:

1 'Blackberry Ice' heuchera (*Heuchera*)

2 'All Gold' Hakone grass (*Hakonechloa macra*)

3 'Maculata' greater periwinkle (*Vinca major*)

4 'Norfolk' friendship plant (*Pilea involucrata*)

5 CATALINA GILDED GRAPE wishbone flower (*Torenia* 'Dancat266')

For shady sites, go for a dramatic impact with high-contrast combinations of colorful foliage, such as purple and yellow.

1. 'BLACKBERRY ICE' HEUCHERA

Heuchera | one 6-inch pot

ALTERNATES: Another heuchera with purple-and-silver leaves, such as 'Amethyst Myst', 'Black Currant', or 'Spellbound', or another 8- to 24-inch-tall, shade-tolerant plant with deep purple or purple-and-silver foliage, such as 'Burgundy Lace' Japanese painted fern (*Athyrium niponicum* var. *pictum*) or 'Chocoholic' bugbane (*Actaea*)

2. 'ALL GOLD' HAKONE GRASS

Hakonechloa macra | one 6- to 8-inch pot

ALTERNATES: Golden Hakone grass (*H. macra* 'Aureola') or another 8- to 12-inch-tall, slender-leaved, shade-tolerant plant with yellow or yellow-variegated, grassy or ferny foliage, such as 'Banana Boat' broadleaf sedge (*Carex siderosticha*), variegated lilyturf (*Liriope muscari* 'Variegata'), or **RITA'S GOLD** Boston fern (*Nephrolepis exaltata* 'Aurea')

3. 'MACULATA' GREATER PERIWINKLE

Vinca major | one 3- to 4-inch pot

ALTERNATES: Another trailing, shade-tolerant plant with solid yellow or yellow-variegated foliage, such as 'Illumination' or '24 Karat' lesser periwinkle (*Vinca minor*) or golden creeping Jenny (*Lysimachia nummularia* 'Aurea')

4. 'NORFOLK' FRIENDSHIP PLANT

Pilea involucrata | one 3- or 4-inch pot

ALTERNATES: Another 3- to 8-inch-tall, shade-tolerant plant with solid purple or purple-and-silver foliage, such as **BLACK SCALLOP** ajuga (*Ajuga reptans* 'Binblasca'), black mondo grass (*Ophiopogon planiscapus* 'Nigrescens'), or wandering Jew (*Tradescantia zebrina*)

5. CATALINA GILDED GRAPE WISHBONE FLOWER

Torenia 'Dancat266' | one 3- to 4-inch pot

ALTERNATES: 'Kauai Lemon Drop' or 'Yellow Moon' wishbone flower (*Torenia fournieri*) or another 3- to 6-inch-tall, trailing or bushy, shade-tolerant plant with yellow flowers, such as 'Eco Dark Satin' or 'Persian Chocolate' dense-flowered loosestrife (*Lysimachia congestiflora*)

MADE FOR SHADE
season by season

Showy foliage gives this shady container high style right from the start, with a balance of harmony and contrast in both colors and textures. The real stars right now are the 'Blackberry Ice' heuchera, with broad, scalloped leaves that are purely purple, veined with black and misted with silver, making a strong contrast to the spiky, bright yellow blades of 'All Gold' Hakone grass.

Wait until nighttime temperatures are consistently above 55°F/13°C before planting your shade container, so the friendship plant doesn't get stunted by chilly weather. Water thoroughly after planting to settle the potting soil around the roots.

EARLY TO MID SUMMER

The 'Blackberry Ice' heuchera and 'All Gold' Hakone grass are still lovely in leaf now, and the smaller plants are starting to have more of a presence. The yellow-and-green foliage of 'Maculata' greater periwinkle picks up the yellow in the Hakone grass, and the bronze-and-silver leaves of the 'Norfolk' friendship plant echo the heuchera's colors. The purple-and-yellow flowers of **CATALINA GILDED GRAPE** wishbone flower join in, too, along with loose spikes of tiny white blossoms on the heuchera.

Give your shade container a good soaking, then let the top inch or so of potting soil dry out before you water again. Also give it a dose of liquid fertilizer every 10 to 14 days. When the periwinkle stems are about 6 inches long, pinch or trim off an inch or so of the end to encourage them to branch.

TIDBITS TIPS AND TRICKS

SHADES OF SHADE. "Partial shade" is generally defined as a site with around 4 to 6 hours of sun a day and "full shade" as a spot with little to no direct sun. Within those two seemingly straightforward categories, however, there are many variations. Five hours of sun during the middle of the day, for instance, is much more intense than the same number of hours from dawn to midday or late afternoon to dusk, particularly in southern regions. So plants that are recommended for partial shade in the North often need full shade in the South — something you need to keep in mind when you're looking for ideas on combinations for shade containers.

The various foliage and flowering features of this shady container combination continue into the later part of the summer. The 'Blackberry Ice' heuchera tends to produce fewer or no new flowers by late summer, but really, you won't miss them, because the blooms of **CATALINA GILDED GRAPE** wishbone flower are so much more colorful. 'All Gold' Hakone grass also flowers around this time, with loose, branching clusters of tiny, greenish blossoms at the tips of the arching stems.

Continue to water and fertilize this five-plant grouping through the rest of the summer, and regularly trim off any dead or damaged leaves. As the heuchera flowers finish, cut off the bloom stems close to the base of the plant. Also trim back any too-long stems on the periwinkle.

All of these plants will look good well into early fall, at least. The 'Norfolk' friendship plant will start to drop leaves once temperatures start dipping into the 50s, and eventually, frost will nip the **CATALINA GILDED GRAPE** wishbone flower. The foliage of 'All Gold' Hakone grass takes on a pinkish blush, then eventually turns brown, but 'Blackberry Ice' heuchera and 'Maculata' greater periwinkle hold their leaves even through the winter.

Keep watering as long as the plants continue to look good. Once the friendship plant and wishbone flower start to decline, pull them out and add them to your compost pile. Transplant the heuchera and Hakone grass to your garden (they should be able to overwinter outdoors from a fall planting in Zone 6 and areas south), or pot them up individually and keep them in a cool place for the winter. Discard or pot up the greater periwinkle.

ON THE MOVE. Shade levels can also change dramatically through the growing season, as deciduous trees leaf out and building, fences, and other structures cast different shadows. So, you may want to keep your shade containers small enough that you can carry them, or else place them on wheeled platforms, so you can easily move them into more or less shade at different times of the year. Signs that plants may need more shade include crispy leaf edges, discolored petals, or browned or pale patches on the foliage. If plants that were flowering freely start blooming less, or if their stems get long and floppy, gradually moving them into more sun can help to get them back into peak form.

Beat THE *Heat*

TOUGH SITES — AROUND POOLS, ON
paved surfaces, and other places exposed to strong,
baking sun — call for tough, heat-tolerant plants. In
hot, dry areas, look for plants that are native to the
southwestern region, such as many ornamental sages
(*Salvia*), or the Mediterranean, such as lavenders
(*Lavandula*) and oleander (*Nerium oleander*). Succulents
and warm-season ornamental grasses also tend to
grow well in hot sites. This gray-toned ball planter
is based primarily on plants from tropical climates,
which are also naturally adapted to heat and humidity,
making them well suited for containers in sultry-
summer areas as long as they get plenty of water.

FULL SUN TO PARTIAL SHADE

CONTAINER: 24" WIDE × 24" HIGH

PLANTS:

1 'Lollipop' Brazilian vervain (*Verbena bonariensis*)

2 'Titan Deep Red' rose periwinkle (*Catharanthus roseus*)

3 'Color Guard' yucca (*Yucca filamentosa*)

4 'Homestead Purple' verbena (*Verbena*)

5 Dwarf chenille plant (*Acalypha reptans*)

When it comes to choosing a container for a hot site, think big. The larger the pot, the slower it will dry out and warm up.

THE 5-PLANT PALETTE

1. 'LOLLIPOP' BRAZILIAN VERVAIN

Verbena bonariensis | one 4- or 6-inch pot

ALTERNATES: 'Little One' Brazilian vervain or another 18- to 24-inch-tall, upright or bushy plant with spiky, purplish flowers, such as 'Goodwin Creek Grey' lavender (*Lavandula*) or Mexican bush sage (*Salvia leucantha*)

2. 'TITAN DEEP RED' ROSE PERIWINKLE

Catharanthus roseus
one 4- or 6-inch pot

ALTERNATES: 'Cora Red' or 'Pacifica Really Red' rose periwinkle or another 12- to 18-inch-tall, bushy, heat-tolerant plant with rosy red to bright pink flowers, such as **ANGELFACE PINK** angelonia (*Angelonia* 'Anpinkim') or 'Acapulco Rose' hummingbird mint (*Agastache*)

3. 'COLOR GUARD' YUCCA

Yucca filamentosa | one 6-inch pot

ALTERNATES: 'Gold Sword' yucca or another 8- to 16-inch-tall, heat-tolerant plant with yellow-variegated leaves, such as variegated foxtail agave (*Agave attenuata* 'Variegata') or 'Samantha' lantana (*Lantana camara*)

4. 'HOMESTEAD PURPLE' VERBENA

Verbena | one 4-inch pot

ALTERNATES: **BABYLON PURPLE** ('Wynena'), 'Imagination',
or **SUPERBENA PURPLE** ('Usbenal25') verbena or another trailing, heat-tolerant plant with purple flowers, such as hardy ice plant
(*Delosperma cooperi*) or **LUSCIOUS GRAPE** lantana (*Lantana camara*
'Robpwpur')

5. DWARF CHENILLE PLANT

Acalypha reptans | one 4-inch pot

ALTERNATES: Another trailing or 4- to 10-inch-tall,
heat-tolerant plant with pink flowers, such as 'Mojave Pink'
or 'Tequila Pink' purslane (*Portulaca grandiflora*) or 'Graffiti
Pink' starflower (*Pentas lanceolata*)

BEAT THE HEAT

season by season

SPRING

The yellow-striped leaves of 'Color Guard' yucca are the stars of this container right from day one, possibly accented with an early bloom or two on the 'Titan Deep Red' rose periwinkle and dwarf chenille plant. 'Lollipop' Brazilian vervain and 'Homestead Purple' verbena are generally just green and leafy at this point.

Wait until nights are consistently above 50°F/10°C, at least, before getting this container started. Put the yucca in place first, then fit the other plants around it. Once they're all in place, water thoroughly to settle them into the potting soil.

EARLY TO MID SUMMER

As the weather begins to heat up, so does this container combination. Joining the dramatic, spiky rosette of 'Color Guard' yucca are the flat, rosy red flowers of 'Titan Deep Red' rose periwinkle; fuzzy, pinkish red tails of dwarf chenille plant; clustered, light purple blooms atop the thin stems of 'Lollipop' Brazilian vervain; and deep purple flowers on the trailing shoots of 'Homestead Purple' verbena.

These plants grow best when the potting soil is moist but not soggy, so water thoroughly when rain is lacking and then let the top inch or so dry out before watering again. Also use a liquid fertilizer every 10 to 14 days. Otherwise, the container doesn't need much attention now.

TIDBITS TIPS AND TRICKS

THE RIGHT CONTAINER FOR HOT SITES. A planter that has thick sides, such as wood or cement, provides extra insulation for tender roots by slowing the heating of the potting soil. You're not limited to those materials, though: any kind of container can work fine in a hot site if you use a somewhat smaller pot as a liner. A liner pot leaves an inch or more of air space between the outer container and the roots, significantly slowing heat transfer.

WATERING WISDOM. Even if you use drought-tolerant plants, container plantings need careful attention to watering, especially at the height of summer. Gathering

MID TO LATE SUMMER

Your "Beat the Heat" container reaches its peak at this point in the growing season, with all the flowering plants in full flower and the 'Color Guard' yucca still serving as a dramatic focal point.

Watering and fertilizing regularly support lush growth and encourage the plants to keep flowering freely during the hottest part of the summer. The dead blossoms of Brazilian vervain, rose periwinkle, and verbena tend to drop off on their own; sweep them up occasionally to keep the area around the container tidy. The fuzzy tails of dwarf chenille plant turn brown and hang on once they're done. New ones will come along and often cover them up, but clipping off the brown tails once a week or so will keep the plant looking fresh. Keep any dead or damaged leaves clipped off, too, and trim back any plants that are starting to crowd out their companions.

FALL

These heat-loving plants keep going even as temperatures cool off in early autumn — even beyond that if frost holds off until mid or late fall.

Keep watering and grooming the grouping as long as the flowering plants are still blooming. Once frost nips them, transplant the yucca to your garden (it should be able to overwinter outdoors from a fall planting as far north as Zone 5). Discard the rest in your compost pile, or, if you live in Zone 7 or a warmer area, put the Brazilian vervain and 'Homestead Purple' verbena in the garden, too; in colder zones, pot them up individually and keep them in a cool place for the winter. Pot up the dwarf chenille plant and put it in a warm, bright spot for the winter. Compost the rose periwinkle; it's easiest to start with new plants each spring.

your pots and planters in one area, near an outdoor faucet, makes the task much easier, because you'll spend less time hauling hoses or watering cans and you'll be less likely to forget one or two. Grouped containers also lend themselves to an automatic (drip) watering system — a great solution if you don't have time to look after your pots and planters every day.

BALCONY
Beauties

WHEN YOUR OUTDOOR LIVING SPACE IS limited to a few square feet, every inch counts. Even if you have room for only one container, you can beautify your balcony, give yourself some privacy, and still have space left over for a place to sit and enjoy the air. Go for a bounty of beautiful blooms or indulge in a mix of flowers, herbs, and edibles, such as this five-plant combination, for fragrance and flavor as well as color. A wheeled planter like this one is easy to move if you want to rearrange your space, or if you want to bring it indoors to hold houseplants in the winter.

FULL SUN TO LIGHT SHADE

CONTAINER: 30" LONG × 15" WIDE × 10" HIGH

PLANTS:

1. 'Osmin' basil (*Ocimum basilicum*)
2. 'Crystal Palace Gem' zonal geranium (*Pelargonium* × *hortorum*)
3. 'Profusion Orange' zinnia (*Zinnia*)
4. SUPERTUNIA ROYAL VELVET petunia (*Petunia* 'Kakegawa S36')
5. 'Tumbling Tom Yellow' tomato (*Solanum lycopersicum*)

1. 'OSMIN' BASIL

Ocimum basilicum
two 3- to 4-inch pots

ALTERNATES: 'Dark Opal' or 'Purple Ruffles' basil or another 12- to 18-inch-tall, upright herb or flowering annual, such as purple culinary sage (*Salvia officinalis* 'Purpurascens') or **ANGELFACE BLUE IMPROVED** angelonia (*Angelonia angustifolia* 'Anbluim')

2. 'CRYSTAL PALACE GEM' ZONAL GERANIUM

Pelargonium × *hortorum* | one 4- to 6-inch pot

ALTERNATES: 'Charity' or 'Vancouver Centennial' zonal geranium or another 12- to 18-inch-tall, bushy annual or herb with colorful flowers or foliage, such as variegated culinary sage (*Salvia officinalis* 'Icterina') or 'Ruby Glow' starflower (*Pentas lanceolata*)

3. 'PROFUSION ORANGE' ZINNIA

Zinnia
two 3- to 4-inch pots

ALTERNATES: Any Profusion Series or Zahara Series zinnia or another 8- to 12-inch-tall, mounded, flowering or foliage annual, such as **INFINITY ORANGE** New Guinea impatiens (*Impatiens hawkeri* 'Visinforimp') or 'Under the Sea Bone Fish' coleus (*Solenostemon scutellarioides*)

4. SUPERTUNIA ROYAL VELVET PETUNIA

Petunia 'Kakegawa S36' | one 3- to 4-inch pot

ALTERNATES: Another petunia or another 6- to 8-inch-tall, loosely mounded to trailing, flowering annual, such as heliotrope (*Heliotropium arborescens*) or **TAPIEN BLUE VIOLET** verbena (*Verbena* 'Sunmaref Tpv')

5. 'TUMBLING TOM YELLOW' TOMATO

Solanum lycopersicum | one 3- to 4-inch pot

ALTERNATES: 'Cherry Falls', 'Peardrops', or 'Tumbling Tom Red' tomato or another 6- to 8-inch-tall, trailing, flowering or fruiting plant, such as 'Gleam Mixed' nasturtium (*Tropaeolum majus*) or 'Berries Galore' strawberry (*Fragaria* × *ananassa*)

BALCONY BEAUTIES
season by season

You'll get some hints of the show to come right from planting time, thanks to the colorful foliage: bright yellow-and-green 'Crystal Palace Gem' zonal geranium and deep purple 'Osmin' basil. The 'Profusion Orange' zinnia and **SUPERTUNIA ROYAL VELVET** petunia may have a new bloom or two now as well.

Basil, in particular, is very sensitive to cold temperatures, so wait until warm weather — when nights are around 55°F/13°C or higher — before planting. Once the plants are in place, water the container to settle the potting soil around the roots. The container might look a little sparse at first, but the plants will fill out quickly and take up all the available space. If you want to give the container a finished look, cover the exposed potting soil with a ½- to 1-inch layer of chopped leaves or shredded bark mulch.

As the weather starts to heat up, these plants jump into vigorous growth. The purple 'Osmin' basil and bright-leaved 'Crystal Palace Gem' zonal geranium continue to add foliage color, joined now by the glowing orange blooms of 'Profusion Orange' zinnia, rich purple trumpets of **SUPERTUNIA ROYAL VELVET** petunia, and tiny yellow, starlike blossoms on the 'Tumbling Tom Yellow' tomato, along with clustered red blooms on the geranium.

Water regularly when rain is lacking to keep the potting soil evenly moist, and apply a liquid organic fertilizer every 7 to 10 days to keep the plants growing steadily. Once the basil plants are at least 6 inches tall, start snipping off the top 1 to 2 inches of each stem (cutting just above a pair of leaves) to encourage side shoots to form. Use the clippings in your kitchen.

TIDBITS TIPS AND TRICKS

CHECK BEFORE YOU PLANT. If you're living in a rental unit, check your lease to see if there are any limitations on how you can decorate your balcony before you invest in pots and plants. There may be restrictions about how much weight you can put out there, whether you're allowed to use hanging baskets, and whether you're permitted to attach containers directly to the balcony railings. Once your containers are in place, be a good neighbor: water carefully so the folks on the balcony below don't get dripped on, and groom your plants often so they're not constantly dropping dead leaves and spent petals.

KEEPING THE BALCONY DRY. To reduce the chance of stains or water damage on your balcony floor, set your pots or planters on saucers to catch any excess

This collection of pretty and productive plants is in prime form right now, filled with beautiful red, orange, and purple flowers on the 'Crystal Palace Gem' zonal geranium, 'Profusion Orange' zinnia, and **SUPERTUNIA ROYAL VELVET** petunia; lush leaves on the 'Osmin' basil and geranium; and tasty yellow fruits on the 'Tumbling Tom Yellow' tomato.

Regular watering is important to keep your balcony garden in great shape through the hottest months. Also keep up with applying a liquid organic fertilizer every 7 to 10 days through the rest of the summer. Every few days, remove any dead or damaged leaves, and pick the dead flowers off the geranium, zinnia, and petunia. Keep snipping off the shoot tips of the basil to keep the plants bushy and get a useful harvest at the same time. Pick the tomatoes as soon as they are fully yellow.

This balcony planter will continue to provide you with both beauty and a useful harvest though early fall, at least. Draping a sheet over the plants at night can help to get them through a light frost or two and extend the growing season a bit. Eventually, freezing temperatures will nip the plants, signaling the end of the spectacle.

Keep watering as long as the plants are still growing, and continue to harvest from the basil and tomato plants. If you want to keep the geranium for next year, take cuttings in early fall, or dig the plant out of the container before frost, pot it up, and set it on a sunny windowsill for the winter. Otherwise, simply pull out all of the frost-killed plants and compost or discard them.

water and fertilizer. It's also a good idea to place them on blocks or wheeled platforms so they're elevated at least an inch or two; that way, the floor beneath them will stay dry.

SELF-WATERING SAVIOR. Balcony plantings tend to lose moisture quickly due to heat and wind, so be sure to check them frequently. If daily watering doesn't fit into your schedule, a "self-watering" container can make the difference between success and disappointment. You'll still need to add water to the built-in reservoir regularly, especially during hot, dry weather, but you'll be able to skip a day or two when things get hectic without sacrificing your beautiful balcony plants.

HUMMINGBIRD
Haven

BIRDS BRING SOUND AND MOVEMENT to your plantings — elements that are easy to forget when you're choosing flowers and foliage for your containers. If you're specifically interested in attracting hummingbirds, there are a couple of tricks you can use to customize your container collections for them. Red flowers, for instance, have long had a reputation for attracting hummingbirds, but orange, yellow, and blue blooms can also work. The shape of the flower tends to be just as important as the color: nectar-rich tubular and trumpet-shaped blossoms tend to be hummingbird magnets.

FULL SUN TO PARTIAL SHADE

CONTAINER: 14" WIDE × 14" HIGH

PLANTS:

1 'Bonfire' begonia (*Begonia boliviensis*)

2 Cigar plant (*Cuphea ignea*)

3 'Gartenmeister Bonstedt' fuchsia (*Fuchsia triphylla*)

4 SUPERBELLS SAFFRON calibrachoa (*Calibrachoa* 'Uscali4134')

5 'Tropical Bronze Scarlet' canna (*Canna*)

2. CIGAR PLANT

Cuphea ignea
one 3- to 4-inch pot

ALTERNATES:
'David Verity' cigar plant or another 8- to 12-inch-tall, bushy plant with nectar-rich flowers, such as 'Profusion Fire' zinnia (*Zinnia*) or 'Vancouver Centennial' zonal geranium (*Pelargonium × hortorum*)

1. 'BONFIRE' BEGONIA

Begonia boliviensis
one 3- to 4-inch pot

ALTERNATES:
BONFIRE CHOC RED ('Nzcfour') begonia or another 6- to 8-inch-tall, low-mounded or trailing plant with nectar-rich flowers, such as golden hardy fuchsia (*Fuchsia magellanica* 'Aurea') or 'Summer Blaze' verbena (*Verbena*)

3. 'GARTENMEISTER BONSTEDT' FUCHSIA

Fuchsia triphylla │ one 3- to 4-inch pot

ALTERNATES: 'Thalia' fuchsia or another 12- to 18-inch-tall, upright plant with bell-shaped or tubular flowers, such as 'Dwarf Red' flowering maple (*Abutilon*) or 'Ruby Glow' starflower (*Pentas lanceolata*)

4. SUPERBELLS SAFFRON **CALIBRACHOA**

Calibrachoa 'Uscali4134' │ one 3- to 4-inch pot

ALTERNATES: **MINIFAMOUS DEEP YELLOW**
('Kleca12224') calibrachoa, or another 6- to 8-inch-tall, low-
mounded to trailing plant with nectar-rich flowers, such as
'Empress of India' nasturtium (*Tropaeolum majus*) or **LITTLE
LUCKY POT OF GOLD** lantana (*Lantana camara* 'Balucgold')

5. 'TROPICAL BRONZE SCARLET' CANNA

Canna │ one 4- to 6-inch pot

ALTERNATES: 'Lucifer' or 'Red Futurity' canna or
another 18- to 24-inch-tall, upright plant with nectar-rich
flowers, such as 'Acapulco Red' hummingbird mint
(*Agastache*) or 'Lady in Red' Texas sage (*Salvia coccinea*)

HUMMINGBIRD HAVEN

season by season

SPRING

The primary spring interest in this collection comes from the dark foliage of 'Gartenmeister Bonstedt' fuchsia and 'Tropical Bronze Scarlet' canna, and the jagged, red-edged green leaves of 'Bonfire' begonia. There may also be a few open blooms on the begonia, cigar plant, fuchsia, and **SUPERBELLS SAFFRON** calibrachoa at planting time.

Early-arriving hummingbirds will be happy to see the first colorful flowers in this container, but don't rush to get this pot out too early. Cold temperatures may stunt some of the plants — particularly the begonia — so wait until nights are sure to stay above 60°F/15°C before setting them outside. Water after planting.

EARLY TO MID SUMMER

Warming weather starts bringing out the blooms in earnest: bright orange on the 'Bonfire' begonia and cigar plant, coral-red 'Gartenmeister Bonstedt' fuchsia, and sunny yellow on **SUPERBELLS SAFFRON** calibrachoa. These vibrant colors show off especially well against the bronzy foliage of the fuchsia and the broad, deep purple leaves of the 'Tropical Bronze Scarlet' canna.

Water regularly if rain is lacking, and apply a liquid fertilizer every 7 to 10 days to encourage steady growth and bloom production. Otherwise, this collection needs little care right now.

TIDBITS TIPS AND TRICKS

HUMMINGBIRD PLANTS FOR SHADE. These five hummingbird plants are suited for full sun in the North, but the begonia and fuchsia, in particular, will appreciate some afternoon shade in warmer climates. Some other plants with flowers that can bring hummers to shady containers include coleus (*Solenostemon scutellarioides*), impatiens (*Impatiens*), browallias (*Browallia*), shrimp plants (*Justicia*), wishbone flowers (*Torenia*), hostas (*Hosta*), and cardinal flower (*Lobelia cardinalis*).

EYE-LEVEL ATTRACTION. Hanging baskets and deck-railing planters are excellent for hummingbird plants, because they make it easy for hummers to access all of

MID TO LATE SUMMER

'Bonfire' begonia and cigar flower are still going strong now, providing a dependable supply of nectar for hungry hummers, and 'Tropical Bronze Scarlet' canna tops off the spectacle with big, bright red blooms. 'Gartenmeister Bonstedt' fuchsia and **SUPERBELLS SAFFRON** calibrachoa may take a bit of a break after their first main flush of bloom, but they're usually back in bloom in late summer.

Ample water and regular fertilizing are especially important now to support these vigorous plants. If you notice some afternoon wilting even when the potting soil is moist, or if some leaves start to develop browned edges, move the container to a spot where it will get some afternoon shade. Keep the plants looking their best with a good grooming every few days. When all of the blossoms in one cluster on a canna stem are finished, clip out that entire stem at the base to make room for new growth. Trim back any particularly long stems on the begonia and fuchsia to keep them in proportion to the rest of the plants and to the container.

FALL

This container collection continues to provide a bounty of beautiful blooms through early fall, at least, providing an abundance of nectar for hummingbirds to feed on before they leave for the season.

Keep watering and grooming your "Hummingbird Haven" as long as the plants are still looking good (usually until frost). If you want to have the begonia and fuchsia for next year, take cuttings in early fall and overwinter them in a warm, bright place. (Don't be alarmed if they drop their leaves; just cut back on watering and be patient, and they'll likely leaf out again in spring.) Or, pull out the cigar plant and calibrachoa, then set the rest of the container in a cool but frost-free place for the winter. Keep the potting soil just moist to overwinter the begonia, fuchsia, and canna in a dormant state.

the flowers without hitting the leaves with their wings — and, they give you a great eye-level view of their activity, too.

SPREADING THE WEALTH. Sometimes a single hummingbird can get very territorial and chase away other hummers from their favorite flowers. To give more of them an opportunity to feed, plant up several containers and place them in different areas — a planter by your front door, a hanging basket outside your kitchen window, and a planter on your back patio, for instance.

BUTTERFLY *Banquet*

FLOWER-FILLED CONTAINER PLANTINGS are a delight for you and your family — and for a variety of beautiful butterflies as well. Increase the odds that these wonderful winged creatures will linger in your yard by providing an abundance of blooms that are particularly rich in both pollen and nectar for them to feed on. Packed with bright flowers in shades of purple, pink, peach, and yellow, this round resin planter would look great on a deck, at poolside, or near a garden bench — really, any sunny spot where there's a place for you to sit and enjoy the fluttering of feeding butterflies.

FULL SUN

CONTAINER: 24" WIDE × 10" HIGH

PLANTS:

1 'Imagination' verbena (*Verbena*)

2 LUCKY PEACH lantana (*Lantana camara* 'Balucpea')

3 SUPERTUNIA SANGRIA CHARM petunia (*Petunia* 'Ustun34803')

4 'Wild Watermelon' littleleaf sage (*Salvia microphylla*)

5 YELLOW CHARM bidens (*Bidens ferulifolia* 'Danyel9')

Clustered blossoms, such as those of verbena and lantana, tend to be especially appealing to butterflies, as do flat, daisy-form flowers, like bidens, because they are easy for the insects to land on and feed from.

1. 'IMAGINATION' VERBENA

Verbena | three 3- to 4-inch pots

ALTERNATES: Moss verbena (*Verbena tenuisecta*) or another 6- to 12-inch-tall, loosely mounded to trailing plant with butterfly-attracting flowers, such as heliotrope (*Heliotropium arborescens*) or 'Wonderland Deep Purple' sweet alyssum (*Lobularia maritima*)

2. LUCKY PEACH
LANTANA

Lantana camara 'Balucpea' one 4- to 6-inch pot

ALTERNATES:
BANDANA PEACH ('Lanz0002') or 'Little Lucky Peach Glow' lantana or another 8- to 16-inch-tall, mounded plant with butterfly-attracting flowers, such as 'Profusion Apricot' zinnia (*Zinnia*) or 'Tip Top Apricot' nasturtium (*Tropaeolum majus*)

3. SUPERTUNIA SANGRIA CHARM PETUNIA

Petunia 'Ustun34803' | one 3- to 4-inch pot

ALTERNATES: **SURFINIA MAGENTA** ('Sunsurfpapu') petunia or another 6- to 12-inch-tall, mounded or trailing plant with butterfly-attracting flowers, such as 'Buddy Purple' globe amaranth (*Gomphrena globosa*) or **SUPERBELLS TRAILING ROSE** calibrachoa (*Calibrachoa* 'Caltrapi')

4. 'WILD WATERMELON' LITTLELEAF SAGE

Salvia microphylla │ one 4- to 6-inch pot

ALTERNATES: Another 18- to 36-inch-tall sage, such as 'Coral Nymph' Texas sage (*Salvia coccinea*), or another bushy plant in that size range with butterfly-attracting flowers, such as **ANGELFACE PINK** angelonia (*Angelonia* 'Anpinkim') or 'Lollipop' Brazilian vervain (*Verbena bonariensis*)

5. YELLOW CHARM BIDENS

Bidens ferulifolia 'Danyel9' │ one 3- to 4-inch pot

ALTERNATES: **GOLDILOCKS ROCKS** ('Bid 719') or **PETER'S GOLD CARPET** ('Goldteppich') bidens or another 6- to 12-inch-tall, loosely mounded to trailing plant with butterfly-attracting flowers, such as 'Profusion Yellow' zinnia (*Zinnia*) or signet marigold (*Tagetes tenuifolia*)

BUTTERFLY BANQUET
season by season

There may be a few early blooms on one or more of these plants when you put them together, giving you a hint of the colors to come — including shades of pink, purple, and yellow — and providing a welcome source of nectar for early-arriving butterflies.

Of these five plants, the lantana is the most sensitive to cold, so wait until nighttime temperatures are at least 55°F/13°C — even better, 60°F/15°C — before putting this container together. (There's not much point in getting an early start, anyway, since butterflies generally don't move around much when temperatures are lower than this.) Water after planting to settle the potting soil around the roots.

Warmer weather really brings out the butterflies, and it also brings out a bounty of blooms in this cheery container: rich purple 'Imagination' verbena, cream-apricot-pink LUCKY PEACH lantana, magenta SUPERTUNIA SANGRIA CHARM petunia, fuchsia-pink 'Wild Watermelon' littleleaf sage, and sunny yellow YELLOW CHARM bidens.

Water regularly when rain is lacking, and apply a liquid organic fertilizer every 7 to 10 days to encourage steady growth and flowering. Other than that, this container needs little care now.

TIDBITS TIPS AND TRICKS

VERTICAL INTEREST. This five-plant collection focuses on a bounty of tiny blooms, creating a cloud of flowers that will act like a magnet for hungry butterflies. If you'd like to give it a bit more height, feel free to add some sort of upright ornament, such as a short metal or wood obelisk or a bit of decorative trellis, to create more vertical impact.

MAKING ROOM FOR HOST PLANTS. When you're planning a butterfly garden, you normally also want to include "host" plants: plants that their larvae can feed on, such as milkweeds (*Asclepias*) for monarchs; rue (*Ruta graveolens*) for giant swallowtails; and parsley (*Petroselinum crispum*), dill (*Anethum graveolens*), and fennel (*Foeniculum vulgare*) for black swallowtails. In the very limited space of a container, though, it's usually not practical to give space to a plant that's just going to get eaten by caterpillars. If you're

MID TO LATE SUMMER

The free-flowering plants in this colorful collection continue to bloom freely through the summer months, so you'll still be enjoying the various shades of pink, purple, and yellow — not to mention the "floating flowers" that come to feed on the abundance of nectar-filled blooms.

Keeping up with watering, especially during hot, dry, or windy conditions, is vital to keeping the plants flowering freely through the summer. Continue to fertilize through late summer, too. Many of these blooms fall off neatly on their own. Trim back any straggly or crowded stems to keep all of the plants in proportion to one another and to the container. The littleleaf sage, especially, can get rather large, so you could cut the whole plant back to about 1 foot in midsummer. Or, every week or so, through midsummer, trim a few of the tallest stems back by a third to a half to encourage bushier growth.

FALL

With good care through the summer, this container collection will continue to delight both you and the butterflies into early fall, at least. In fact, the 'Wild Watermelon' littleleaf sage tends to flower most freely as cooler weather returns, so there'll be no shortage of nectar to give winged visitors energy for the trip to their winter resting spots.

Continue watering as long as the plants are still growing and flowering. Light frost will nip the lantana, but the other plants can keep going until a freeze. Covering the container with a sheet on the night of the first light frost can help to keep the whole collection looking good for a while longer; or, snip out the frost-killed bits of lantana and enjoy the rest of the flowers for a few more days or weeks. Once freezing temperatures call a halt to the growing season, pull out all of the plants and add them to your compost pile.

dedicated to providing a welcoming habitat for butterflies, put those and other host plants in your yard, or dedicate a whole container to them and put it in a less visible spot, and keep the showy flowers that attract adult butterflies front and center.

WATERING HOLE. Butterflies also appreciate a source of water, and it's very easy to provide that in even a small space. Simply fill a pot saucer or shallow dish with sand or soil, place it next to your butterfly container, and keep it moist to create a puddling place for them to drink.

Kid ATTRACTION

JUST LIKE IN-GROUND GARDENS, container plantings can be so much more than just beautiful blooms: plants can also be fragrant or flavorful, with leaves that are lovely to touch or silly-looking flowers that simply make you smile. These are all features to keep in mind when you want to plan a planter that's sure to grab a young person's attention, or if you enjoy a touch of whimsy in container combinations for any age. This wooden half-barrel planter includes two easy and interesting edibles, along with please-pet-me leaves and quirky blooms that are sure to attract attention throughout the growing season.

FULL SUN

CONTAINER: 18" WIDE × 16" HIGH

PLANTS:

1 'Jumbo Virginia' peanut (*Arachis hypogaea*)

2 'Silky Fleece' lamb's ears (*Stachys byzantina*)

3 Eyeball plant (*Acmella oleracea*)

4 'Micro Tom' tomato (*Solanum lycopersicum*)

5 Dwarf chenille plant (*Acalypha reptans*)

After harvesting, leave your peanut plant — roots and all — in a dry place for a week or so. Then, enjoy your peanuts!

135

1. 'JUMBO VIRGINIA' PEANUT

Arachis hypogaea
one 4-inch pot or one packet of seeds

ALTERNATES: Another 12- to 24-inch-tall, bushy plant with edible parts, such as 'All Blue' potato (*Solanum tuberosum*) or ground cherry (*Physalis pruinosa*); showy flowers, such as 'Sunny Smile' sunflower (*Helianthus annuus*); or attractive fruits, such as 'Easter Egg' ornamental eggplant (*Solanum ovigerum*)

2. 'SILKY FLEECE' LAMB'S EARS

Stachys byzantina | one 4- or 6-inch pot

ALTERNATES: Common lamb's ears or another 6- to 12-inch-tall plant with "touchable" leaves, such as peppermint geranium (*Pelargonium tomentosum*), dwarf lady's mantle (*Alchemilla erythropoda*), or sensitive plant (*Mimosa pudica*)

3. EYEBALL PLANT

Acmella oleracea | one 4-inch pot

ALTERNATES: A 12- to 18-inch-tall, bushy plant with fragrant flowers, such as chocolate cosmos (*Cosmos atrosanguineus*), heliotrope (*Heliotropium arborescens*), or Spanish lavender (*Lavandula stoechas*), or with "touchable" flowers or foliage, such as bunny tails grass (*Lagurus ovatus*) or Mexican feather grass (*Stipa tenuissima*)

4. 'MICRO TOM' TOMATO

Solanum lycopersicum | two 4-inch pots

ALTERNATES: Another 6- to 8-inch-tall, bushy plant with edible parts, such as alpine strawberry (*Fragaria vesca*), 'Easter Egg' radishes (*Raphanus sativus*), or rounded 'Atlas', 'Paris Market', or 'Thumbelina' carrot (*Daucus carota* var. *carota*)

5. DWARF CHENILLE PLANT

Acalypha reptans | two 4-inch pots

ALTERNATES: Another 3- to 8-inch-tall, bushy or trailing plant with fragrant leaves or pretty flowers, such as 'Chocolate' mint (*Mentha* × *piperita*), 'Lime' thyme (*Thymus* × *citriodorus*), or **PINK PANDA** strawberry (*Fragaria* 'Frel')

KID ATTRACTION
season by season

SPRING

The primary interest of this planter right now comes from the fun of planting and the fuzzy foliage of the 'Silky Fleece' lamb's ears, and possibly an early bloom or two on the eyeball plant and dwarf chenille plant.

Wait until night temperatures are consistently 60°F/15°C or higher to pot up your container. Or, instead of an already started plant, plant a few peanut seeds in early to mid spring. Keep the pot in a warm place (70 to 80°F/21 to 27°C is ideal), and give it lots of light once the sprouts are up. Once nights are warm, gradually expose the pot to more sunshine over the period of a week or so, then add it to the center of the container. Water the completed container to settle the plants into the potting soil. It might look a little sparse at first, but don't be tempted to add more plants, because the peanut, in particular, will need plenty of space later.

EARLY TO MID SUMMER

As the weather warms up, your kids' container will begin to fill out quickly. 'Jumbo Virginia' peanut and 'Silky Fleece' lamb's ears contribute lovely leaves (light green on the peanut and silver-furred on the lamb's ears), accented with the red-dotted yellow globes and bronzy green leaves of eyeball plant, the starry yellow blossoms of 'Micro Tom' tomato, and the fluffy pink tails of dwarf chenille plant.

Water this planter regularly when rain is lacking (let the top inch or so of potting soil dry out in between), and use a liquid fertilizer every 7 to 14 days to encourage steady growth. Pinch or clip the browned old blooms off the eyeball plant and dwarf chenille plant to keep them looking their best. If aphids attack the eyeball plant, squash them with your fingers and/or clip off the infested shoots.

TIDBITS TIPS AND TRICKS

CREATIVE CONTAINERS. Take your five-plant kids' garden to the next level with a quirky container, such as a child-sized wheelbarrow or an old wagon or toy box. Or use a collection of smaller repurposed containers, such as Easter baskets, outgrown shoes, or toy watering cans, to hold individual plants. If it has some sort of hole to let excess water drain away (or if you can add holes), it's fair game for planting.

PEANUT LOVE. Peanuts (*Arachis hypogaea*) are one of those plants that everyone should try at least once, just for the experience of watching their interesting growth pattern. Once flowering begins, large-seeded types like 'Jumbo Virginia' need about 3 more months to produce fully mature peanuts. If you live where frost is common by late September, it's worth hunting for a smaller-seeded variety, such as 'Early Spanish',

MID TO LATE SUMMER

The eyeball plant and dwarf chenille plant are filled with flowers now, and the leaves of the 'Silky Fleece' lamb's ears are still eminently pettable. 'Jumbo Virginia' peanut should be in bloom by midsummer, but you won't notice the small yellow flowers unless you look closely at the base of the plant. As the flowers finish, they send a slender shoot down into the potting soil; that's where the new peanuts will develop through the rest of the summer. 'Micro Tom' tomato will likely have green fruits forming by midsummer, and they'll ripen into orangey red, cherry-sized fruits a few weeks later.

Keep up with regular watering and fertilizing, and continue to remove the finished flowers on the eyeball plant and dwarf chenille plant. You may also need to trim off some leaves or even whole shoots on those plants as well, to keep them from crowding out the peanut.

FALL

This kids' collection keeps growing into early fall, at least, with flowers still on the eyeball plant and dwarf chenille plant, and an abundance of silvery foliage on the 'Silky Fleece' lamb's ears. The peanut will have loads of leaves now, too, though they'll eventually turn yellow as the season progresses.

Keep up with watering (though not fertilizing) as long as your container planting looks good. If nights start to get frosty but your peanut is still growing, move the container to a protected spot, or cover it with an overturned bucket or box on chilly nights to keep it growing as long as possible. When you're ready to dismantle the container, discard the eyeball plant and dwarf chenille plant on your compost pile, and transplant the lamb's ears to your garden. Then pull out the peanut plant and shake the potting soil off the roots.

which will ripen several weeks earlier. Either way, you should be able to get at least a few fully formed peanuts, as well as some immature ones, from a September harvest — enough to make the experience worthwhile.

TOOTHACHE PLANT. One glance at the rounded, dark-dotted blooms of *Acmella oleracea* (also known as *Spilanthes oleracea*), and it's easy to see how it gets the common names eyeball plant and peekaboo plant. You won't be able to guess where its other name — toothache plant — comes from by looking at it, but you can if you nibble on a bit of a leaf or flower bud. You'll notice a couple of intriguing reactions: one, a brief numbness where you chew on it, and two, a fizzy sort of tingling sensation in your whole mouth. It usually goes away after just a few minutes, but it's an interesting experience while it lasts.

A MINI *Meadow*

IF YOUR STYLE TENDS TO LEAN TOWARD country casual, a meadow-style container could be a perfect fit for you. In nature, a meadow is mostly native grasses, accented with a few flowers. In the garden, a meadow feature tends to be more "naturalistic": it includes both grasses and flowers, but not always native species, and with more emphasis on colorful blooms. The result has a flowing, informal look that's still at home in a suburban or even urban setting. This mini-meadow combination, contained in a clay-colored cube planter, offers months of unfussy beauty and also creates a bit of backyard habitat for birds, butterflies, and beneficial insects.

FULL SUN

CONTAINER: 20" LONG × 20" WIDE × 20" HIGH

PLANTS:

1 'Arizona Apricot' blanket flower (*Gaillardia* × *grandiflora*)

2 'Kobold' blazing star (*Liatris spicata*)

3 Mexican feather grass (*Stipa tenuissima*)

4 'Prairie Splendor' purple coneflower (*Echinacea purpurea*)

5 'Shenandoah' switch grass (*Panicum virgatum*)

A natural-looking or rustic planter makes a perfect complement to a naturalistic container combination.

141

1. 'ARIZONA APRICOT' BLANKET FLOWER

Gaillardia × grandiflora | two 4- to 6-inch pots

ALTERNATES: 'Mesa Peach' blanket flower or another 8- to 16-inch-tall, mounded or bushy annual or perennial with orangey or yellow, daisy-form flowers, such as 'Little Goldstar' orange coneflower (*Rudbeckia fulgida* var. *sullivantii*) or 'Zagreb' coreopsis (*Coreopsis verticillata*)

2. 'KOBOLD' BLAZING STAR

Liatris spicata
two 6-inch pots

ALTERNATES:
Another 18- to 24-inch-tall, upright annual or perennial with spiky, purple-blue to purplish or rosy pink flowers, such as **ANGELFACE BLUE** angelonia (*Angelonia angustifolia* 'Anblauzwei'), 'East Friesland' salvia (*Salvia nemorosa*), or 'Raspberry Nectar' hummingbird mint (*Agastache*)

3. MEXICAN FEATHER GRASS

Stipa tenuissima | two 3- to 4-inch pots

ALTERNATES: Another 12- to 18-inch-tall, mound-forming ornamental grass, such as 'Piglet' fountain grass (*Pennisetum alopecuroides*) or prairie dropseed (*Sporobolus heterolepis*)

4. 'PRAIRIE SPLENDOR' PURPLE CONEFLOWER

Echinacea purpurea | two 4- to 6-inch pots

ALTERNATES: 'Kim's Knee High' or **PIXIE MEADOWBRITE** ('CBG Cone 2') purple coneflower or another 18- to 24-inch-tall, upright, summer-flowering perennial with pinkish or purplish, daisy-form or flat-topped flowers, such as **GRAND PARADE** bee balm (*Monarda* 'Acrade') or 'Saucy Seduction' yarrow (*Achillea*)

5. 'SHENANDOAH' SWITCH GRASS

Panicum virgatum | one 6-inch pot

ALTERNATES: 'Cheyenne Sky' switch grass or another 18- to 30-inch-tall, upright ornamental grass, such as 'Gold Bar' or 'Little Kitten' miscanthus (*Miscanthus sinensis*) or 'Prairie Blues' little bluestem (*Schizachyrium scoparium*)

A MINI MEADOW
season by season

SPRING

If you're starting with greenhouse-grown plants, there may be a few early flowers on the 'Arizona Apricot' blanket flower and 'Prairie Splendor' coneflower. The foliage of the 'Kobold' blazing star, Mexican feather grass, and 'Shenandoah' switch grass contribute textural interest, too. If you're using outdoor-grown starts, they may be just starting to emerge from their individual pots at planting time.

All of these perennials can tolerate cold temperatures, as long as they are used to being outside and not fresh out of a greenhouse. If they've been growing inside, gradually expose them to increasingly long periods outside over the course of a week or so. Plant them in the container once danger of frost has passed. Water to settle the plants into the potting soil. If you wish, add a 1-inch-deep layer of chopped leaves, shredded bark, or other organic mulch to give the container a finished look.

EARLY TO MID SUMMER

Your meadow container will start to fill out quickly as the weather gets warmer, with lots of fresh-looking foliage accented by the first main flush of orange-shaded yellow flowers on the 'Arizona Apricot' blanket flower, and possibly some rosy pink blooms on the 'Prairie Splendor' purple coneflower as well as purplish pink spikes on the 'Kobold' blazing star.

Water regularly when rain is lacking, letting the top 2 inches of potting soil dry out in between waterings, and apply a liquid fertilizer every 10 to 14 days. Clip off the rounded balls left when the blanket flower blossoms drop their petals to encourage the plants to produce new blooms.

TIDBITS TIPS AND TRICKS

MINI PLANTS. Flowers and grasses in natural meadows tend to be on the tall side, often reaching eye level or even higher — too tall to fit the proportions of most planters, and prone to flopping and looking messy. Fortunately, there are more compact cultivars of many of the most beautiful meadow plants, reaching half the size of the native species or even smaller. These shorter selections are ideal for bringing the simple beauty of a wide country meadow to a few square feet of container space. Instead of wild switch grass (*Panicum virgatum*), for instance, which may reach to 6 feet or more in full bloom, consider 'Shenandoah', which tops out at just 4 feet when mature, or 'Cheyenne Sky', which reaches barely 3 feet by the end of the growing season.

By midsummer, this container is reaching its peak, with an abundance of daisy-form blooms on 'Arizona Apricot' blanket flower and 'Prairie Splendor' purple coneflower and fuzzy-looking bloom spikes on 'Kobold' blazing star rising above the elegantly arching green leaves of the Mexican feather grass. 'Shenandoah' switch grass creates a vertical accent in the center, with its green blades developing red tips in midsummer and airy flower heads emerging at the top of the plant in late summer.

Keep up with watering now, and fertilize again once or twice before late summer. Keep clipping the dead blooms off the blanket flower. Cut off the finished purple coneflower blossoms (snip just above the uppermost leaf or bud on the stem), to encourage rebloom, or leave them to develop into dark seed heads that will attract finches and other backyard birds. These winged visitors also enjoy feeding on the fluffy seed heads of the 'Kobold' blazing star.

Along with a few lingering blooms on the 'Arizona Apricot' blanket flower and 'Prairie Splendor' purple coneflower, the mix of interesting seed heads and graceful grasses make for a splendid fall show that lasts well into fall — and even into winter in warmer areas.

Keep watering during dry spells as long as the plants are still growing. In Zone 7 and south, these perennials should be able to overwinter in the container, so you can enjoy the display as long as possible. If you want to keep the plants for next year in colder areas (most are hardy to Zone 5, at least), dismantle the planting in early to mid fall. Transplant the blanket flower, purple coneflower, blazing star, and switch grass to your garden; pot up the Mexican feather grass and keep it in a cool place for the winter.

FILLING IN THE GAPS. Your mini-meadow container may look a little sparse at first, but don't be tempted to add additional perennials, because these plants will need all of the space in just a few weeks. Instead, consider adding some small pots of spring bulbs that are already in bud or bloom for a quick burst of bloom. They'll turn yellow and go dormant in early summer, around the time that the meadow perennials are growing together; then you can transplant the bulbs to your garden in fall. Or, you could instead tuck in some small cool-season annuals, such as sweet alyssum (*Lobularia maritima*) or violas (*Viola*), for late spring color, then pull them out in early summer, when the perennials fill out.

POND *in a* POT

NO NEED TO GIVE UP VALUABLE GROUND space to enjoy a beautiful water garden. Even a relatively small container can hold a variety of wonderful water plants, creating an intriguing and unexpected feature that fits perfectly on a deck or patio. A container water garden is also a great way to get your feet wet, so to speak, if you are considering adding a full-sized water garden to your yard but want to get some practice first. The key to success is choosing plants that are suited to the size of your chosen pot, so they'll grow in balance with each other and need minimal maintenance. This cobalt blue resin bowl is home to five fuss-free plants that thrive in shallow water.

FULL SUN TO PARTIAL SHADE

CONTAINER: 18" WIDE × 8" HIGH

PLANTS:

1 Water calla (*Zantedeschia aethiopica*)

2 Variegated Japanese iris (*Iris ensata* 'Variegata')

3 Corkscrew rush (*Juncus effusus* 'Spiralis')

4 Water lettuce (*Pistia stratiotes*)

5 Red-stemmed parrot's feather (*Myriophyllum brasiliensis*)

Floating plants, such as water lettuce (*Pistia stratiotes*), don't need planting at all: just drop them into water that's at least a few inches deep and they'll sit right on the surface.

147

1. WATER CALLA

Zantedeschia aethiopica
one 4- to 6-inch pot

ALTERNATES:
Another 18- to 30-inch-tall, upright aquatic plant with showy flowers, such as blue pickerel rush (*Pontederia cordata*), bog lily (*Crinum americanum*), or common arrowhead (*Sagittaria latifolia*)

2. VARIEGATED JAPANESE IRIS

Iris ensata 'Variegata' | one 4- to 6-inch pot

ALTERNATES: Another 12- to 18-inch-tall, upright aquatic plant with colorful, spiky foliage, such as variegated sweet flag (*Acorus calamus* 'Variegatus'), variegated society garlic (*Tulbaghia violacea* 'Variegata'), or 'Red Dragon' rice (*Oryza sativa*)

4. WATER LETTUCE

Pistia stratiotes | one plant

ALTERNATES: Another 4- to 10-inch-tall, upright or rosette-forming aquatic plant with interesting foliage, such as variegated water celery (*Oenanthe javanica* 'Flamingo') or water hyacinth (*Eichornia crassipes*)

3.CORKSCREW RUSH

Juncus effusus 'Spiralis' one 4-inch pot

ALTERNATES: Another 6- to 12-inch-tall, upright aquatic plant with colorful foliage, such as chameleon plant (*Houttuynia cordata* 'Chameleon') or variegated dwarf papyrus (*Cyperus albostriatus* 'Variegatus')

5. RED-STEMMED PARROT'S FEATHER

Myriophyllum brasiliensis | one bunch or 4-inch pot

ALTERNATES: Common parrot's feather (*Myriophyllum aquaticum*) or another aquatic plant with floating foliage, such as 'Crystal Confetti' water pennywort (*Hydrocotyle sibthorpioides*) or mosaic plant (*Ludwigia sedioides*)

POND IN A POT

season by season

SPRING

The primary interest in this container comes from foliage, not flowers, so it will look lovely from the minute all of the plants are in place.

While most of the plants in this container can tolerate some chill, water lettuce needs warm water, so wait until temperatures remain consistently above 60°F/15°C to get your water garden started. Fill the container with water, then wait at least a full day to let any chlorine dissipate and give the water a chance to warm up. Slowly lower the potted plants, until the bottom of each one rests on the bottom of the container, then place the water lettuce on the surface so its roots are dangling into the water.

EARLY TO MID SUMMER

The variety of leaf shapes in this combination offers plenty to catch the eye: large and arrow-shaped on the water calla; narrow and spiky on the iris; slender and spiraled on the corkscrew rush; flat, ridged, and arranged in rosettes on the water lettuce; and tiny and feathery, in brushy whorls, on the red-stemmed parrot's feather. You might get a purple flower or two on the iris by around this time, or a white flower on the water calla, but since you'll be starting with relatively small plants, they may not be large enough to flower the first year.

No need to worry about watering this container, except for occasionally adding a bit more water to replace whatever's lost to evaporation. Use a fertilizer meant for aquatic plants, applied at the rate and frequency recommended on the package. Any algae that shows up should disappear on its own as the plants settle in and begin to shade the surface of the water.

TIDBITS TIPS AND TRICKS

SIZING UP YOUR POT. Most containers are best suited for plants that are well adapted to shallow water. If you have a container that's roughly 6 to 10 inches deep, you can set potted bog plants and marginals on the bottom, and their crown will be at about the right level. Water lilies (*Nymphaea*), on the other hand, tend to need relatively large pots (at least 18 inches deep), but small kinds, such as 'Chromatella', can adapt to life in containers just a foot or so deep.

DISCOURAGING MOSQUITOES. Water gardens do more than just look pretty: they provide a welcome source of water for birds and beneficial insects as well. Keep in mind, though, that like other sources of standing water, container water gardens can provide a place for mosquitoes to breed. In any size container, you can use the natural control *Bacillus thuringiensis* var. *israelensis* (*Bti*), which is available in commercial

MID TO LATE SUMMER

The interplay of foliage colors and textures evident earlier in the season continues to provide the primary interest in this container water garden now: a cooling sight that's very welcome during the hottest part of the summer.

Add more water as needed to keep the container filled almost to the rim, and continue to fertilize according to the product label directions. Clip off any dead or damaged leaves, and, if necessary, remove some rosettes of the water lettuce and/or some of the red-stemmed parrot's feather foliage if the planter is getting too crowded.

FALL

Your container water garden should continue to be attractive into early fall, at least, so you can continue to appreciate the variety of intriguing leaves for a while longer.

As temperatures begin to dip below 60°F/15°C, the water lettuce will turn yellow or brown. In most areas, it's easiest to treat it, the water calla, and the parrot's feather as annuals and discard them in your trash at the end of the season. (Do not discard aquatic plants in your compost or anywhere that they could get into natural waterways.) Transplant the variegated Japanese iris and corkscrew rush to your garden — they'll also grow in moist garden soil as far north as Zone 4 — or lift their pots and set them in a cool place for the winter. Dump the remaining water out of the container and scrub and rinse the inside to remove any clinging debris, then store the pot for the winter.

products such as Mosquito Bits and Mosquito Dunks. Simply sprinkle or drop them in the water to control the larvae without any harm to people, pets, birds, or fish.

AVOIDING INVASIVE SPECIES. Several popular water-garden plants, including water hyacinth (*Eichornia crassipes*), common parrot's feather (*Myriophyllum aquaticum*), and water lettuce (*Pistia stratiotes*), can spread quickly and become seriously invasive if they enter in-ground ponds, lakes, and waterways; for that reason, it is forbidden to sell them in some areas. For a complete list of plants that may be banned in your state, check the State Noxious Weed Lists directory at http://plants.usda.gov/java/noxiousDriver. If any of the plants suggested for this container are forbidden in your state, then choose alternates from among the many other available aquatic plants.

MAGIC *in* MINIATURE

TABLETOP GARDENS, ALSO CALLED DISH gardens or fairy gardens, include the same elements as full-sized landscapes: upright "trees"; lower, bushy "shrubs"; and ground-hugging "ground covers"; plus ornamental elements such as paths, benches, tables, trellises, and gazebos. Planning and planting a tabletop garden is a particularly wonderful project for children or folks with limited mobility, and the finished project makes a charming centerpiece for a porch or patio table. This miniature green-and-white garden can tolerate several hours of direct sun, but morning light is usually better than strong afternoon sun, which can speedily dry out the soil in the relatively shallow ceramic pot.

PARTIAL SHADE

CONTAINER: 10" LONG × 6" WIDE × 3" HIGH

PLANTS:

1 False aralia (*Schefflera elegantissima*)

2 Variegated artillery plant (*Pilea microphylla* 'Variegata')

3 Buddhist pine (*Podocarpus macrophyllus*)

4 'Mini White' nerve plant (*Fittonia argyroneura*)

5 Baby's tears (*Soleirolia soleirolii*)

Broad, relatively shallow containers (like this bonsai pot) work well for tabletop gardens, because they give you opportunities to try out different arrangements of the tree, shrub, and ground cover levels and leave room for accessories, too.

1. FALSE ARALIA

Schefflera elegantissima
one 3-inch pot

ALTERNATES:
Another 6- to 8-inch-tall
plant with a treelike or
vase-shaped form and
deep green leaves, such
as weeping fig (*Ficus
benjamina*) or dwarf
parlor palm (*Chamaedorea
elegans* 'Bella')

2. VARIEGATED ARTILLERY PLANT

Pilea microphylla 'Variegata' | one 3-inch pot

ALTERNATES: Another 4- to 6-inch-tall plant with a treelike
form and white-variegated foliage, such as dwarf snowbush
(*Breynia disticha* 'Nana'), 'Snowflake' ming aralia (*Polyscias fruticosa*), or variegated serissa (*Serissa foetida* 'Variegata')

3. BUDDHIST PINE

Podocarpus macrophyllus
one 3-inch pot

ALTERNATES:
Another 2- to 4-inch-tall,
upright or bushy plant
with spiky or fine-
textured green leaves,
such as 'Itsy Bitsy'
English ivy (*Hedera
helix*), dwarf myrtle
(*Myrtus communis*
'Compacta'), dwarf
mondo grass (*Ophiopogon
japonicus* 'Nana'),
or miniature rush
(*Eleocharis radicans*)

4. 'MINI WHITE' NERVE PLANT

Fittonia argyroneura | one 2-inch pot

ALTERNATES: Another white- or pink-veined nerve plant
or another 2- to 3-inch-tall, rosette-forming plant with silver,
white, and/or pink in the leaves, such as 'Tricolor' strawberry begonia (*Saxifraga stolonifera*), or white, pink, or purple flowers, such as a miniature African violet (*Saintpaulia
ionantha*)

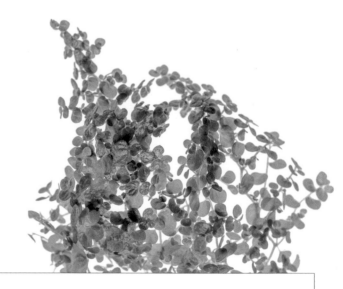

5. BABY'S TEARS

Soleirolia soleirolii | one 3- or 4-inch pot

ALTERNATES: Another ground-hugging, creeping plant
with green foliage, such as Corsican mint (*Mentha requienii*)
or Irish moss (*Sagina subulata*)

MAGIC IN MINIATURE
season by season

SPRING

Who needs flowers? The beauty of this miniature garden comes from the intricate interplay of plant heights and forms, as well as leaf shapes, textures, and colors, so you'll enjoy the effect right from planting day.

All of these plants prefer to stay on the warm side (normal room temperatures are ideal), so don't be in a hurry to put this container outside for the season. You can get it started any time, as soon as you have the plants on hand, but wait until temperatures are sure to stay above 60°F/15°C before you move it outdoors. Water after planting, then add the trellis and garden chair.

EARLY TO MID SUMMER

The variety of plants in this tabletop garden gives this small container the impact of a well-planned larger landscape. The tall false aralia serves the role of a shade tree, while the heavily branched, spreading variegated artillery plant mimics a flowering tree, and the clump of Buddhist pine resembles a small evergreen shrub. Closer to the ground, the spreading 'Mini White' nerve plant resembles a foliage-filled flower bed, while baby's tears hugs the ground, creating a lawnlike effect.

Regular watering is critical, because the soil in this shallow container can dry out quickly. Apply a dose of liquid fertilizer once or twice a month. In windy weather, or if storms are predicted, move your tabletop garden to a sheltered spot or bring it indoors until calmer conditions return.

TIDBITS TIPS AND TRICKS

MORE MINI PLANTS. When you're looking for plants to fill your tabletop planter, check out displays of terrarium plants at your favorite greenhouse or garden center. These tiny treasures come in a wide range of shapes and colors and will fit easily in a small pot that you can put outside in some shade for the summer and bring indoors for the winter. If you'd prefer to display your miniature garden in sun, consider dwarf conifers and other small, slow-growing evergreens for the tree- and shrub-form plants and little alpines or hardy perennial ground covers for the lowest level. Or, create the three-level effect with a variety of hardy or tender succulents instead.

MID TO LATE SUMMER

Lovely leaves continue to provide interest through the growing season, ranging from deep green on the false aralia and Buddhist pine to bright green on the baby's tears and white-veined green on the 'Mini White' nerve plant. The tiny leaves of variegated artillery plant are so heavily marked with white that there's barely any green at all. They're lightly blushed with pink, too, particularly at the shoot tips.

Keep up with the watering and occasional fertilizing, and with protecting your tiny tabletop garden during stormy summer weather. There's very little other maintenance to do besides removing any dead or damaged leaves and occasionally trimming the artillery plant to maintain its treelike form.

FALL

Every good thing about this tabletop garden continues into autumn and all winter as well. That's a big return from a tiny container.

Keep up with watering (but not fertilizing) through the fall and winter, though you'll need to do it much less often now. Once nighttime temperatures start dipping into the low 60s, bring the container indoors and keep it in a warm, bright spot or put it under a plant light for the winter. Do a bit of light trimming occasionally to keep the plants well-shaped and in proportion to each other. If you find that the plants are getting too big for the container, pot them up individually and start over with smaller new plants in spring.

MINI ACCESSORIES. Some greenhouses and garden centers are catching on to the fairy-garden trend and carrying a selection of accessories, such as tiny fences and arbors, to complete your tiny landscape. For more options, check out the offerings of miniature furniture and model train layout supplies at local craft and toy stores, or search for "miniature garden accessories" or "fairy garden accessories" online. You may be able to find other finishing touches in your yard or around your house. For a woodland theme, for instance, look for weathered twigs or bits of bark or moss; for a seaside garden, use sand for a path and tiny shells as accents.

SALAD *on* DECK

A COLLECTION OF COLORFUL CONTAINERS and ornamental edibles makes for a display that's a treat for the eye as well as for the palate, supplying months of fresh salad fixings right outside your door. This grouping includes crisp and colorful lettuces and other greens, plus oniony common chives (*Allium schoenoprasum*), tasty tomatoes (*Solanum lycopersicum*), and edible flowers, in a set of brightly colored, food-grade plastic tubs with handles that make them easy to move as needed.

FULL SUN

CONTAINERS: 18" WIDE × 13" HIGH;
15" WIDE × 12" HIGH; 12" WIDE × 9" HIGH

PLANTS:

1 'Silvery Fir Tree' tomato (*Solanum lycopersicum*)

2 'Alaska' nasturtium (*Tropaeolum majus*)

3 Common chives (*Allium schoenoprasum*)

4 'Galactic' lettuce (*Lactuca sativa*)

5 Mesclun

Besides keeping them handy for watering and harvesting, growing greens and other beautiful and flavorful salad crops in containers keeps them raised above the ground, so they don't get splashed with mud in rainy weather.

1. 'SILVERY FIR TREE' TOMATO

Solanum lycopersicum
one 4- to 8-inch pot

ALTERNATES:
Another compact,
determinate tomato,
such as 'Bush Early
Girl', or a bush-type
cucumber (*Cucumis
sativus*), such as
'Picklebush'

2. 'ALASKA' NASTURTIUM

Tropaeolum majus │ six 4-inch pots or one packet of seeds

ALTERNATES: Another bushy nasturtium, such as 'Dwarf Jewel
Mix'; another edible flower, such as johnny jump ups
(*Viola tricolor*) or pot marigold (*Calendula officinalis*); or radishes
(*Raphanus sativus*)

3. COMMON CHIVES

Allium schoenoprasum
one 4- to 6-inch pot

ALTERNATES:
Another herb with
flavorful leaves, such
as garlic chives (*Allium
tuberosum*), chervil
(*Anthriscus cerefolium*), or
salad burnet (*Poterium
sanguisorba*

4. 'GALACTIC' LETTUCE

Lactuca sativa | one 6-cell pack

ALTERNATES: Another leaf lettuce with red or red-and-green leaves, such as 'Outredgeous' or 'Flashy Butter Oak', or a red-leaved mustard (*Brassica juncea*), such as 'Ruby Streaks' or 'Scarlet Frills'

5. MESCLUN

one packet of seeds

ALTERNATES: Any salad green, such as arugula (*Eruca sativa*), mizuna (*Brassica rapa* Nipposinica Group), or mixed lettuces (*Lactuca sativa*)

SALAD ON DECK

season by season

SPRING

A week or two before your usual last frost date, sow the mesclun seeds in the smallest container. Start harvesting when the leaves are 3 to 4 inches tall, cutting with scissors about 1 inch above the base of the plants. Start the medium-sized container around the same time, setting the chives in the center and spacing the lettuce transplants evenly around the edge. Start harvesting the lettuce when the plants are 4 to 6 inches tall, and harvest the chives after 3 to 4 weeks. In the largest container, you can plant the nasturtium transplants or seeds around the edge as soon as all danger of frost has passed, but wait until nights stay above 50°F/10°C before setting the tomato plant in the center.

Once your crops are growing, water regularly when rain is lacking, and add a liquid fertilizer every 7 to 10 days. If the weather gets chilly at night (below freezing for the small and middle container; below 50°F/10°C for the largest one), bring the containers into a sheltered spot at night until it warms up again.

EARLY TO MID SUMMER

'Galactic' lettuce, common chives, and mesclun are all producing lots of leaves now, so keep harvesting as needed. When the 'Alaska' nasturtiums begin to bloom, snip off some of the buds and open blooms (and some of the peppery-flavored leaves, if you wish) for fresh use. 'Silvery Fir Tree' tomato is beautiful and bushy now, with some yellow flowers and developing fruits appearing by midsummer.

Keep watering and fertilizing regularly. When the lettuce and mesclun plants start tasting bitter or growing upright stems, pull them out and add them to your compost pile. Add a bit more potting soil where they were growing. If it's still early summer, replant with seeds or transplants for a midsummer harvest. In early summer, add a cage or stakes to the largest container to keep the tomato plant from sprawling later on.

TIDBITS TIPS AND TRICKS

MUSINGS ON MESCLUN. Mesclun isn't one specific crop; rather, it's a term that applies to a mix of leafy greens meant to be picked when young and tender for salads. It usually includes a few varieties of leaf lettuce (*Lactuca sativa*); beyond that, there are different mixes to suit different tastes. If you like spicy flavors, look for mixes that include zippy greens like arugula (*Eruca sativa*), mizuna (*Brassica rapa* Nipposinica Group), and mustard (*Brassica juncea*). Greens that are slightly bitter, such as endive (*Cichorium endivia*) and chicory (*Cichorium intybus*), make an interesting mix with sweet, tender lettuces. For lots of color, choose a mix with both green and red lettuces, plus red orach (*Atriplex hortensis* var. *rubra*), red-leaved beets (*Beta vulgaris* Conditiva Group), and multicolored Swiss chard (*B. vulgaris* Cicla Group).

MID TO LATE SUMMER

If you replanted in early summer, 'Galactic' lettuce and mesclun are leafy now and available for harvest as needed, along with the chive foliage. The rounded green fruits of 'Silvery Fir Tree' ripen to orangey red over a period of about 3 weeks in mid to late summer, making a beautiful display against the plant's silvery green leaves and the variegated leaves and red, golden, or orangey flowers of the 'Alaska' nasturtiums. Pick the tomato fruits when they're fully colored for slicing into salads, and clip some nasturtium buds, flowers, and/or leaves as desired.

Continue watering and fertilizing all three containers through late summer. Replant the mesclun and lettuce at the end of the summer. Remove the tomato plant when you harvest the last fruit. Fill its space with lettuce or other leafy greens, or just let the nasturtiums fill in.

FALL

You'll enjoy the good looks and good flavors of the 'Galactic' lettuce, common chives, 'Alaska' nasturtiums, and mesclun through early fall until frost.

Once freezing weather nips the plants, transplant the chives to your garden (they should be fine in Zone 4 and areas south from a fall planting) and toss the rest of the plants into your compost pile.

SOWING MESCLUN. Fill the smallest container to within an inch of the rim with moistened potting soil, and scatter mesclun seeds evenly over the surface (try to get them ½ to 1 inch apart). Cover them with about ¼ inch of potting soil, firm the surface lightly by pressing it with your fingers, and sprinkle regularly with water to keep the soil evenly moist. It can take anywhere from 3 to 14 days for the seeds to sprout.

COAXING CHIVES TO FLOWER. When you start with a pot of common chive (*Allium schoenoprasum*) seedlings, you probably won't get flowers the first year. But if you move the plant to your garden for the winter and then transplant part or all of the clump back to a container in spring, you'll get a bounty of beautiful (and edible) pink flowers from late spring into summer.

HERBS *on the* WINDOWSILL

COOKING WITH FRESH HERBS IS A REAL treat, and you can't get much fresher than herbs you've picked right outside your door. Growing your favorite kitchen herbs in a pot or planter on your deck or patio keeps the leaves clean and makes it easy to grab a few sprigs any time you need them throughout the growing season. And when they're growing vigorously, you can harvest the abundance for drying or freezing and continue to enjoy their flavors through the winter months. This tin window box planter includes a variety of savory herbs that work well with beef, poultry, soups, and stews, as well as tomato-based dishes.

FULL SUN TO LIGHT SHADE

CONTAINER: 24" LONG × 10" WIDE × 8" HIGH

PLANTS:

1 Common thyme (*Thymus vulgaris*)

2 'Hot & Spicy' oregano (*Origanum vulgare*)

3 'Lockwood de Forest' rosemary (*Rosmarinus officinalis*)

4 'Pesto Perpetuo' basil (*Ocimum × citriodorum*)

5 'Triple Curled' parsley (*Petroselinum crispum* var. *crispum*)

Using a self-watering window box can help to cut down on watering chores, but you'll still need to water the plants regularly for the first month or so, until the roots spread out.

1. COMMON THYME

Thymus vulgaris
one 3- to 4-inch pot

ALTERNATES:
Another 6- to 10-inch-tall, bushy culinary herb,
such as lemon thyme (*Thymus × citriodorus*), sweet marjoram (*Origanum majorana*), or summer savory (*Satureja hortensis*)

2. 'HOT & SPICY' OREGANO

Origanum vulgare | one 3- to 4-inch pot

ALTERNATES: Greek oregano (*Origanum vulgare* subsp. *hirtum*) or another 4- to 8-inch-tall, bushy or trailing culinary herb, such as salad burnet (*Poterium sanguisorba*) or winter savory (*Satureja montana*)

3. 'LOCKWOOD DE FOREST' ROSEMARY

Rosmarinus officinalis
one 3- to 4-inch pot

ALTERNATES:
IRENE ('Renzels') or creeping rosemary ('Prostratus') or another 4- to 10-inch-tall, bushy or trailing culinary herb, such as common chives (*Allium schoenoprasum*) or French tarragon (*Artemisia dracunculus*)

4. 'PESTO PERPETUO' BASIL

Ocimum × citriodorum | one 3- to 4-inch pot

ALTERNATES: Sweet basil or 'Purple Ruffles' basil
(*Ocimum basilicum*) or another 12- to 18-inch-tall, bushy
culinary herb, such as culinary sage (*Salvia officinalis*) or
'Fernleaf' dill (*Anethum graveolens*)

5. 'TRIPLE CURLED' PARSLEY

Petroselinum crispum var. *crispum* | three 3- to 4-inch pots

ALTERNATES: Italian parsley (*P. crispum* var. *neapoli-
tanum*) or another 8- to 16-inch-tall, bushy culinary herb,
such as chervil (*Anthriscus cerefolium*) or cilantro (*Coriandrum
sativum*)

HERBS ON THE WINDOWSILL
season by season

You'll enjoy your beautiful container herb garden right from planting time, thanks to the various leaf colors: grayish green common thyme and 'Hot & Spicy' oregano, deep green 'Lockwood de Forest' rosemary, brilliant emerald 'Triple Curled' parsley, and green-cream-white 'Pesto Perpetuo'.

Most of these herbs can tolerate a lot of cold, but the basil may be stunted if it gets chilled, so wait until nights stay above 50°F/10°C before planting this container. Water thoroughly after planting to settle the soil around the roots. Add a ½- to 1-inch mulch of sphagnum moss, gravel, or shredded bark, if desired, to keep the potting soil from splashing up onto the leaves.

As your culinary herbs settle in, fill out, and start to grow together, you'll really appreciate the contrasting forms and foliage textures: bushy, tiny-leaved common thyme and frilly 'Triple Curled' parsley; trailing, fuzzy 'Hot & Spicy' oregano and needlelike 'Lockwood de Forest' rosemary; and very upright, smooth-leaved 'Pesto Perpetuo' basil. The common thyme may also produce tiny white to pinkish white flowers now; they're not very showy, but bees enjoy them, so be careful when harvesting.

Water regularly when rain is lacking to keep the potting soil moist but not soggy. Add a liquid organic fertilizer every 10 to 14 days to encourage vigorous, leafy growth. Feel free to clip some leaves or shoot tips of your tasty herbs to use fresh. If you wish, cut the whole thyme plant by a third to a half when the flowers start to open, and dry the clippings for winter cooking.

TIDBITS TIPS AND TRICKS

FAST-GROWING HERBS. Once you've tried a single five-plant container of culinary herbs, there's a good chance that you'll want to expand your collection. It's easy to find room for individual pots of fast-growing annual herbs, such as cilantro (*Coriandrum sativum*), chervil (*Anthriscus cerefolium*), and 'Fernleaf' dill (*Anethum graveolens*). Sow their seeds directly into the pots in spring, and you'll be able to start harvesting in just a few weeks. When those plants are done, pull them out, add fresh potting soil, and sow again for a fall crop.

FISH-FRIENDLY HERBS. If you frequently cook fish, consider tweaking your container choices to include some complementary herbs. Lemony herbs, such as lemon balm (*Melissa officinalis*) and lemongrass (*Cymbopogon citratus*), are handy for adding a citrusy flavor to your fish if you don't happen to have fresh lemons on hand. Anise-flavored

While the abundant and flavorful foliage remains the focus of this container, there may still be some flowers on the common thyme if you didn't cut back the whole clump earlier. You may also see some clusters of tiny pinkish white blossoms on the 'Hot & Spicy' oregano now.

Watering is especially important during hot, dry weather to keep your herbs vigorous and productive. Also keep fertilizing until late summer. Harvest leaves as you need them for fresh use. To keep the container looking good, regularly remove any dead or damaged foliage. Clip or pinch back the longest shoots of the basil to keep the plant a pleasing bushy shape; use the clippings fresh or purée them with olive oil and freeze them for winter use. Cut the oregano back by half when flowers start to form and dry the cut pieces for storage.

Your culinary herb collection will continue to look good and produce a useful harvest through early fall. Eventually, chilly nights (below 50°F/10°C) will slow down the basil, and the first frost will kill it, but the other herbs will keep growing for a while longer.

Continue to water and groom your herbs as long as they are growing in the container. To finish the growing season with a final generous harvest, cut all of the tops just above the potting soil and freeze or dry them for later use; then pull out the remains and compost them. If you'd rather extend your supply of fresh herbs as long as possible, bring the entire container (or the individually potted-up herbs) into a warm, bright spot and pinch or clip off the leaves or shoots as you need them.

herbs, such as dill, fennel (*Foeniculum vulgare*), and French tarragon (*Artemisia dracunculus*), are also wonderful for grilled, steamed, or baked fish.

SAVE THE CATERPILLARS! Herbs usually aren't seriously bothered by pests, but you may see light green caterpillars with black and yellow markings feeding on your parsley. Don't be tempted to kill them, because they are the larval form of beautiful black swallowtail butterflies. Instead, clip off the leaf they're currently feeding on and place them on a clump of parsley, dill, or fennel somewhere else in your yard.

A POT of TEA

A CHARMING CONTAINER FILLED WITH FIVE sweet and tasty herbs is a treat for any tea lover. You can enjoy the leaves and/or flowers of single herbs; combine two or more herbs for a blend of flavors; or use one or more herbs to liven up your favorite black, green, or white tea. Growing your favorite tea herbs in a container keeps them close to the house for easy harvesting. They stay much cleaner, too, since they're off the ground and won't get splashed with mud during rainy weather. This copper-toned metal tub yields a variety of minty, citrusy, and fruity flavors, along with stevia (*Stevia rebaudiana*) for use as a natural sweetener.

FULL SUN TO LIGHT SHADE

CONTAINER: 20" LONG × 14" WIDE × 10" HIGH

PLANTS:

1. CRAZY SWEET stevia (*Stevia rebaudiana* 'Ac G11a11')
2. German chamomile (*Matricaria recutita*)
3. Lemongrass (*Cymbopogon citratus*)
4. Spearmint (*Mentha spicata*)
5. Variegated peppermint (*Mentha × piperita* 'Variegata')

1. CRAZY SWEET STEVIA

Stevia rebaudiana 'Ac G11a11' | one 4- to 6-inch pot

ALTERNATES: Regular stevia or another 12- to 24-inch-tall, upright herb with flavorful leaves or flowers, such as 'Pink Lace' bee balm (*Monarda didyma*) or lemon basil (*Ocimum* × *citriodorum*)

2. GERMAN CHAMOMILE

Matricaria recutita
one 3- to 4-inch pot

ALTERNATES: Another 10- to 18-inch-tall, upright herb with flavorful flowers, leaves, or seeds, such as Roman chamomile (*Chamaemelum nobile*), anise (*Pimpinella anisum*), or coriander (*Coriandrum sativum*)

3. LEMONGRASS

Cymbopogon citratus | one 4- to 6-inch pot

ALTERNATES: Another 18- to 30-inch-tall, upright herb with flavorful leaves or flowers, such as lemon verbena (*Aloysia triphylla*), pineapple sage (*Salvia elegans*), or rose geranium (*Pelargonium graveolens*)

4. SPEARMINT

Mentha spicata
one 4- to 6-inch pot

ALTERNATES:
Another 12- to 18-inch-tall, upright to some-what trailing herb with flavorful leaves or flowers, such as catnip (*Nepeta cataria*), mojito mint (*Mentha × villosa*), or orange mint (*M. × piperita* f. *citrata*)

5. VARIEGATED PEPPERMINT

Mentha × piperita 'Variegata'
one 3- to 4-inch pot

ALTERNATES:
Common or 'Chocolate' peppermint or another 8- to 12-inch-tall, upright to somewhat trailing herb with flavorful leaves or flowers, such as pineapple mint (*Mentha suaveolens* 'Variegata'), variegated lemon balm (*Melissa officinalis* 'Variegata'), or varie-gated lemon thyme (*Thymus × citriodorus* 'Variegata')

A POT OF TEA

season by season

SPRING

Some of these herbs are very cold-tolerant, but young lemongrass and stevia plants don't like to be chilled, so it's best to wait until nighttime temperatures stay above 60°F/15°C before planting, or else bring the planted container indoors at night until the weather is dependably warm. Water after planting to settle the potting soil around the roots. If you wish, add a ½- to 1-inch layer of sphagnum moss, gravel, or shredded bark as a mulch to help prevent the potting soil from splashing up on the leaves.

This container may look a little sparse at planting time, but don't be disappointed: these vigorous herbs need the space to fill out later. In the meantime, just enjoy the interplay of interesting leaves: spiky lemongrass, lacy German chamomile, bright green **CRAZY SWEET** stevia and spearmint, and cream-and-green variegated peppermint.

EARLY TO MID SUMMER

The various leaf textures and shades of green are the primary source of visual interest right now. These herbs fill out quickly as the weather warms up, so it's fine to snip some leaves from the **CRAZY SWEET** stevia, lemongrass, spearmint, or variegated peppermint once or twice a week for fresh use in your tea.

Water regularly if rain is lacking to keep the potting soil evenly moist (but not soggy), and apply a liquid organic fertilizer every 7 to 10 days. The spearmint and stevia are likely to be growing steadily by midsummer, so feel free to trim the longest stems by a third to a half; that will encourage them to branch and give you a nice harvest to use fresh or to dry.

TIDBITS TIPS AND TRICKS

BREW TIME! Ready to brew up a cup of home-grown herbal tea? Figure on 2 to 3 tablespoons of fresh herbs for each cup of water. Boil the water, pour it over the herbs in a teapot, and cover the top. Let the tea steep for 5 to 10 minutes, then try a sip to see if you're pleased with the flavor; if you'd like it stronger, let the rest brew for a few more minutes. Strain out the herbs, then enjoy your herbal tea plain or sweetened to taste.

MAKING FLAVORED SUGAR. Try a twist on a more traditional sweetener for your tea with homemade geranium sugar. It's usually made with rose geranium (*Pelargonium graveolens*), but other scented geraniums (*Pelargonium*) will work, too, and all of them make beautiful container plants. For each cup of granulated sugar, use about 10 whole, clean leaves. Let the leaves air-dry for several days, rub them with your fingers to

MID TO LATE SUMMER

Flowers now join the various interesting leaf colors and textures in this container planting: spikes of light purple blooms on the peppermint and pinkish white blossoms on the spearmint, and small, white-petaled, yellow-centered daisies on the German chamomile.

Keep watering and fertilizing to keep the herbs vigorous and productive. Regularly remove any dead or damaged leaves, and snip off any browned tips on the lemongrass. When you notice flower spikes forming on the spearmint, cut the entire plant back by about half to get bushy new growth for fall. Use those trimmings for tea, along with the leaves and flowers of the variegated peppermint, the leaves of the lemongrass and stevia, and the flowers of the German chamomile.

FALL

Loads of leafy growth keep your tea container looking lush well into autumn, accented with the delicate daisies of German chamomile. **CRAZY SWEET** stevia may also produce clusters of white flowers in early fall.

Continue watering as long as the herbs are still growing; no need to fertilize, though. Cut off the stevia flowers to promote leafy growth. Before the arrival of freezing temperatures, gather your final harvest. Cut the spearmint, peppermint, and stevia stems back to about 3 inches. Dry the mint clippings whole. Dry the stevia leaves and tender shoot tips. Clip off and dry the flowers of the German chamomile. Cut the lemongrass stems close to the base of the plant and freeze them for winter use. Transplant the spearmint and peppermint to your garden (they're generally hardy to Zone 5, at least). It's usually easiest to start with new lemongrass and stevia plants each spring. Add the German chamomile to your compost pile.

release the oils, and then layer the sugar and leaves in a clean, dry glass jar. Cover tightly, and let the jar sit for at least a week. Remove the leaves and enjoy the flavored sugar in beverages or baking. (If the sugar has gotten clumpy, break it up again in a blender or food processor before using or storing it in an airtight container.)

SWEET STEVIA. If you've never used stevia before, try adding just one or two fresh leaves for each cup of water when you brew other herbs for tea; add more next time if you want the flavor to be sweeter. Regular stevia tends to have an aftertaste that some people like and others dislike. If you're in the latter group, don't give up on stevia altogether until you've given the selection **CRAZY SWEET** ('Ac G11a11') a try, because it seems to have little to no residual flavor beyond the sweetness.

Bursting WITH Berries

WHAT A TREAT TO BE ABLE TO PICK JUICY, sun-warmed fruits right outside your door! When you grow fruiting plants in containers, you can place them in just the right light conditions and keep them close to your house for easy watering, harvesting, and maintenance. Where space is limited, focus on fruits that aren't readily available at the grocery store, or that are at their best when just picked, such as most berries. This set of three metal planters holds a variety of annual, perennial, and woody plants that produce succulent, tasty berries, with a bonus of pretty flowers and colorful foliage.

FULL SUN TO PARTIAL SHADE

CONTAINERS: 14" LONG × 14" WIDE × 21" HIGH
11" LONG × 11" WIDE × 16" HIGH
9" LONG × 9" WIDE × 12" HIGH

PLANTS:

1 'Raspberry Shortcake' raspberry (*Rubus idaeus*)

2 'White Pine' pineberry (*Fragaria × ananassa*)

3 'Top Hat' blueberry (*Vaccinium*)

4 'Golden Alexandria' alpine strawberry (*Fragaria vesca*)

5 'Aunt Molly's' ground cherry (*Physalis pruinosa*)

Ground cherries are relatives of tomatillos and have an unusual sweet-tart flavor. The plants are so productive that you can get enough for a pie from just one plant.

1. 'RASPBERRY SHORTCAKE' RASPBERRY

Rubus idaeus │ one 8-inch pot

ALTERNATES: A dwarf fig (*Ficus carica*), such as 'Petite Negra';
a dwarf mulberry (*Morus alba*), such as 'Issai'; or a trellised passion
flower (*Passiflora edulis*), such as 'Possum Purple'

2. 'WHITE PINE' PINEBERRY

Fragaria × *ananassa* │ four plants

ALTERNATES: Another pineberry, such as 'Natural Albino',
or an everbearing red strawberry, such as 'Eversweet' or
'Mara des Bois'

3. 'TOP HAT' BLUEBERRY

Vaccinium
one 8-inch pot

ALTERNATES:
Another compact blueberry, such as **JELLY BEAN** ('Zf06-179') or **PEACH SORBET** ('Zf06-043'), or dwarf pomegranate (*Punica granatum* 'Nana')

4. 'GOLDEN ALEXANDRIA' ALPINE STRAWBERRY

Fragaria vesca
four 3- to 4-inch pots

ALTERNATES:
Another alpine strawberry, such as red 'Baron Solemacher' or 'Mignonette' or cream to white 'Pineapple Crush' or 'Yellow Wonder'

5. 'AUNT MOLLY'S' GROUND CHERRY

Physalis pruinosa │ one 4-inch pot

ALTERNATES: Any other ground cherry or another 6- to 24-inch-tall fruiting plant, such as cape gooseberry (*Physalis peruviana*), wonderberry (*Solanum burbankii*), or alpine strawberry (*Fragaria vesca*)

BURSTING WITH BERRIES

season by season

You'll probably need to buy the pineberry plants from a mail-order nursery, so place your order in early to mid spring. Get your containers started once all danger of frost has passed. Make sure you buy a 'Raspberry Shortcake' raspberry plant that has some woody brown stems, because those are the ones that will produce fruit later in the summer. It's a quick spreader, so leave it in its nursery pot; set it into the center of the largest planter, add more potting soil around it, and place the pineberry plants at the corners. They'll probably be bare-root when you receive them; set the crown (the point where the roots come together) at the surface and fully cover the roots, and look for new growth within a week or so.

For the middle planter, remove the blueberry from its pot and set it in the center, then place the alpine strawberry plants in the corners. Set one started plant of 'Aunt Molly's' ground cherry into the center of the smallest pot once the weather stays above 50°F/10°C.

'Top Hat' blueberry continues to flower into early summer, then leafs out as the berries begin to form. 'Golden Alexandria' alpine strawberry is still blooming now, too, joined by yellow-centered white flowers on the 'White Pine' pineberry and 'Raspberry Shortcake' raspberry. 'Aunt Molly's' ground cherry will likely be in bloom by midsummer, with tiny yellow flowers, though they're not very showy. Your harvest will start now: first the alpine strawberry fruits when they turn red, then the pineberries when they turn white or pinkish, and then the raspberries when they're red and come off easily in your hand.

Thoroughly water all three planters regularly. In the largest container, make sure you water both the inner pot with the raspberry as well as along the sides, where the pineberries are growing. Use a liquid fertilizer every 10 to 14 days.

TIDBITS TIPS AND TRICKS

MAKING A STRAWBERRY GARDEN. It would be easy to create a container fruit garden with nothing but different types of strawberries (*Fragaria*). June-bearers produce only one main crop a year, in late spring to early summer: nice if you'd like to enjoy a good quantity of berries over a few weeks. Everbearing (also known as day-neutral) strawberries, too, produce generously in late spring to early summer; after taking a break for a few weeks, they then continue to bloom and fruit lightly through the rest of the growing season. Pineberries (*Fragaria* × *ananassa*) are interesting for something different: they're not particularly productive, and their fruits are small (about quarter-sized), but they're white to pale pink and dotted with red seeds. Alpine strawberries (*Fragaria vesca*) bloom and produce tiny but flavor-packed berries pretty much continuously from late spring to frost.

The fruits keep coming into midsummer, at least. The 'White Pine' pineberries and 'Raspberry Shortcake' raspberries will taper off, but the 'Top Hat' blueberry fruits then ripen over a period of several weeks. 'Golden Alexandria' alpine strawberry may take a break for a few weeks during the hottest part of the summer. When husks drop from the 'Aunt Molly's' ground cherry, bring them inside. When the husks turn fully yellow to brown, usually within a few days, open the husk to reveal the golden yellow, ripe fruit.

Continue to water your fruit containers through this period, but stop fertilizing in late summer. Pay special attention to the smallest planter, because it can dry out quickly as the plant gets big. If the ground cherry gets too large or floppy, feel free to trim it back by about a third. Remove the runners of the pineberry plant, if you wish, or leave some or all of them to enjoy the cascading effect. Regularly trim off any dead or discolored leaves.

While 'Raspberry Shortcake' raspberry, 'White Pine' pineberry, and 'Top Hat' blueberry are unlikely to produce more fruit after mid to late summer, their rich green leaves should still look good into fall and may even take on some reddish colors as the weather gets cool. 'Golden Alexandria' alpine strawberry and 'Aunt Molly's' ground cherry continue to produce flowers and fruit until frost.

Keep watering as long as the plants are growing. Frost will kill the ground cherry plant; add it to your compost pile. In Zone 7 and warmer areas, transplant the remaining plants to your garden, if you wish. Elsewhere, move the medium-sized and large planters to a cool place, such as an unheated garage, in late fall, and water occasionally during the winter.

SELECTING CROSS-POLLINATORS. Some blueberries (*Vaccinium*), some pineberries, and some other fruiting plants need cross-pollination — at least two plants of different, compatible varieties — to produce a good (or any) harvest. It's not necessary to have both plants in the same pot: the pollinizer can be in different container, or even in a bed or border close to the potted plant. For pineberries that need a pollinizer, like 'Natural Albino', red-fruited 'Sonata' seems to be a good match, and it's not hard to find room for one plant of that variety for each four pineberry plants. If you want to grow blueberries but have room for only one plant, look for a variety that's described as "self-pollinating" or "self-fruitful," such as JELLY BEAN ('Zf06-179'), PEACH SORBET ('Zf06-043'), or 'Top Hat'.

JUST RIGHT
for Night

IF YOU'RE AWAY FROM HOME ALL DAY, you may not even get outside before dark, let alone have much time to appreciate your beautiful containers. You can still get a great deal of pleasure from your pots and planters, though, if you include some classic elements of evening gardens, such as night-blooming flowers and plants that have white or pale blooms and leaves to catch even the smallest bit of light. A container filled with plants that have these features — such as this octagonal cast stone planter packed with white flowers and white-variegated leaves — is an ideal addition to a deck or balcony where you like to relax after the day's chores are done.

FULL SUN TO PARTIAL SHADE

CONTAINER: 20" WIDE × 16" HIGH

PLANTS:

1. Variegated angel's trumpet (*Brugmansia suaveolens* 'Variegata')
2. EVERCOLOR EVEREST Japanese sedge (*Carex oshimensis* 'Carfit01')
3. FROSTY KNIGHT sweet alyssum (*Lobularia maritima* 'Inlbupripr')
4. 'Betty White' bacopa (*Sutera*)
5. Lemon balm (*Melissa officinalis*)

Pinch off the shoot tips of the lemon balm every few weeks to keep the plant low and bushy.

2. EVERCOLOR EVEREST JAPANESE SEDGE

Carex oshimensis 'Carfit01' | two 4-inch pots

ALTERNATES: 'Evergold' Japanese sedge or another 6- to 10-inch-tall, spiky or bushy plant with white-variegated foliage, such as 'Spark Plug' sedge (*Carex phyllocephala*) or **SILVER DRAGON** creeping lilyturf (*Liriope spicata* 'Gin-ryu')

1. VARIEGATED ANGEL'S TRUMPET

Brugmansia suaveolens 'Variegata' | one 6- to 10-inch pot

ALTERNATES: Another angel's trumpet with white-variegated foliage, such as 'Peaches and Cream' or 'Snowbank', or solid green foliage, such as 'Charles Grimaldi'; or another 3- to 6-foot-tall, shrubby plant with pale, night-scented flowers, such as lady of the night (*Brunfelsia gigantea*) or 'Dwarf Deciduous White' plumeria (*Plumeria rubra*)

3. FROSTY KNIGHT SWEET ALYSSUM

Lobularia maritima 'Inlbupripr' | one 4- or 6-inch pot

ALTERNATES: Another sweet alyssum, or another 4- to 6-inch-tall, bushy or trailing plant with white-variegated leaves and/or white flowers, such as **MEZOO TRAILING RED** Livingstone daisy (*Dorotheanus bellidiformis* 'Mesbicla') or dwarf or variegated Natal plum (*Carissa macrocarpa* 'Nana' or 'Variegata')

4. 'BETTY WHITE' BACOPA

Sutera | one 4-inch pot

ALTERNATES: **GIANT SNOWFLAKE** ('Danova906'), **GULLIVER WHITE** ('Dangul14'), or another white-flowered bacopa, or another trailing annual with small, white flowers, such as **MINIFAMOUS DOUBLE WHITE** calibrachoa (*Calibrachoa* 'Kleca13242')

5. LEMON BALM

Melissa officinalis | one 4-inch pot

ALTERNATES: Another 6- to 12-inch-tall, bushy plant with lemon- or mint-scented foliage, such as catnip (*Nepeta cataria*), pennyroyal (*Mentha pulegium*), or spearmint (*Mentha spicata*)

JUST RIGHT FOR NIGHT

season by season

SPRING

You'll enjoy many of this container's special features from the very first day (and evening): the white- to cream-variegated leaves of the variegated angel's trumpet, **EVERCOLOR EVEREST** Japanese sedge, and **FROSTY KNIGHT** sweet alyssum; the white flowers, too, on the sweet alyssum, as well as on the 'Betty White' bacopa; and the lemon-scented leaves of the lemon balm.

All five of these plants can tolerate a fair bit of chill, but it's best to wait until temperatures stay consistently above 45°F/7°C, at least, to get your evening container started. And, make sure you've gradually exposed all of the indoor-grown plants to outdoor conditions before you put them outside for good. Water after planting to settle the potting soil around the roots.

EARLY TO MID SUMMER

The various variegated residents in this container continue to add visual interest as the growing season progresses, along with the small but abundant blooms of 'Betty White' bacopa and tiny, clustered, scented blossoms of **FROSTY KNIGHT** sweet alyssum. There are plenty of bright green lemon balm leaves now, so feel free to pinch some off to release their citrusy scent. You'll also see some small white flowers on the lemon balm, but they're not very showy. That distinction goes to the giant-sized, pendulous white blooms of the variegated angel's trumpet, which may make their first appearance right now, releasing their perfume in the evening.

Water frequently, and apply a liquid fertilizer every 10 to 14 days to encourage lush growth and flowering. Around midsummer, trim the lemon balm back by a half to two-thirds to keep it lower and bushier. (Use the trimmings in hot or iced tea.)

TIDBITS TIPS AND TRICKS

PERFUMING THE NIGHT AIR. For flowers that do double duty, consider container plants with beautiful blooms that are also delightfully fragrant at night. In a large container, for instance, place some sort of vertical trellising to the center to support a moonflower (*Ipomoea alba*), a fast-growing annual vine with large white blossoms that swirl open in the evening to release their rich scent. Four-o'clock (*Mirabilis jalapa*) is another annual that opens later in the day, with an abundance of perfumed blooms in a range of colors. A couple of other wonderful choices for late fragrance include night-blooming jasmine (*Cestrum nocturnum*) — it's powerfully scented, so one small plant is all you need — and lady of the night (*Brunfelsia*), with white to cream blossoms that are lightly fragrant during the day and more intensely perfumed after dark.

MID TO LATE SUMMER

All of the good things about this five-plant collection — foliage, flowers, *and* fragrance — continue through the rest of the summer to enhance your evenings in your outdoor living space. Even if the variegated angel's trumpet doesn't always have blossoms — it tends to bloom off and on through the growing season — it will always have its beautiful leaves, and there will still be other blooms to appreciate.

The variegated angel's trumpet, in particular, will need lots of water and frequent fertilizing to keep growing and flowering through summer's heat. If you find that its leaves are drooping even with regular watering, consider moving your evening container to a shadier spot for the hottest part of the summer. Remove any dead or discolored leaves and flowers regularly so the plants always look their best.

FALL

Continue to enjoy the good looks and delicious scents of this five-plant planting through early autumn evenings — even into mid- or late fall if mild weather tends to linger in your area.

Eventually, frosty weather will call a halt to your evening container display. Transplant the Japanese sedge and lemon balm to your garden (the sedge should be hardy to Zone 6 and the lemon balm to Zone 4), and toss the sweet alyssum and bacopa on your compost pile. It's worth trying to keep the variegated angel's trumpet for a container or your garden next year. Unless you have a greenhouse or large sunroom — it will continue to grow and flower in warm, bright conditions — the easiest way to overwinter it is to haul the container into a cool but frost-free place (such as an unheated garage or basement) and keep it fairly dry. Most or all of the leaves will drop, but the stems should survive.

SILVERY SENSATIONS. White-variegated foliage is a perfect complement to white flowers in an evening container — and so are silvery leaves. Some sparkling silvers that work well in pots and planters include trailing 'Silver Falls' silver ponyfoot (*Dichondra argentea*) and licorice plant (*Helichrysum petiolare*), and bushy dusty miller (*Senecio cineraria*) and 'Parfum d'Ethiopia' wormwood (*Artemisia*).

LIVING *Perfume*

IN A GARDEN, FRAGRANCE IS A PLEASURE; in a container, it's sheer delight. Growing scented plants in pots and planters lets you bring them right up close to your house, where you can easily enjoy a sniff any time you pass by. And, you'll hardly even have to bend over, since their raised placement puts them much closer to nose level. Scented container plantings are particularly nice in a sheltered spot — on a porch, perhaps, or a deck or patio that's bounded by walls on two sides — so scents can linger instead of getting swept away by a breeze. This cubic, brown-glazed container holds a variety of hardy and tender plants that are lovely to look at and pleasingly perfumed as well.

FULL SUN TO PARTIAL SHADE

CONTAINER: 14" LONG × 14" WIDE × 14" HIGH

PLANTS:

1. FIONA SUNRISE jasmine (*Jasminum officinalis* 'Frojas')
2. PLATINUM BLONDE lavender (*Lavandula angustifolia* 'Momparler')
3. Lemon verbena (*Aloysia triphylla*)
4. White heliotrope (*Heliotropium arborescens* 'Alba')
5. Variegated calamint (*Calamintha grandiflora* 'Variegata')

Lemon verbena can get quite large, so don't hesitate to clip off some of the shoots to keep the plant in proportion to the container. Bring those clippings into the kitchen: they're delicious in hot or iced tea!

1. FIONA SUNRISE JASMINE

Jasminum officinalis 'Frojas' | one 6-inch pot

ALTERNATES: Arabian jasmine (*Jasminum sambac*) or star jasmine (*J. nitidum*), or another climber with fragrant flowers, such as bridal bouquet (*Stephanotis floribunda*) or corkscrew vine (*Vigna caracalla*)

2. PLATINUM BLONDE LAVENDER

Lavandula angustifolia 'Momparler' | one 4-inch pot

ALTERNATES: **SILVER EDGE** English lavender (*L. angustifolia* 'Walvera') or 'Linda Ligon' French lavender (*L. dentata* 'Variegata'), or another 12- to 18-inch-tall, bushy plant with fragrant, variegated foliage, such as 'Snowy Nutmeg' geranium (*Pelargonium fragrans*) or 'French Lace' geranium (*P. crispum*)

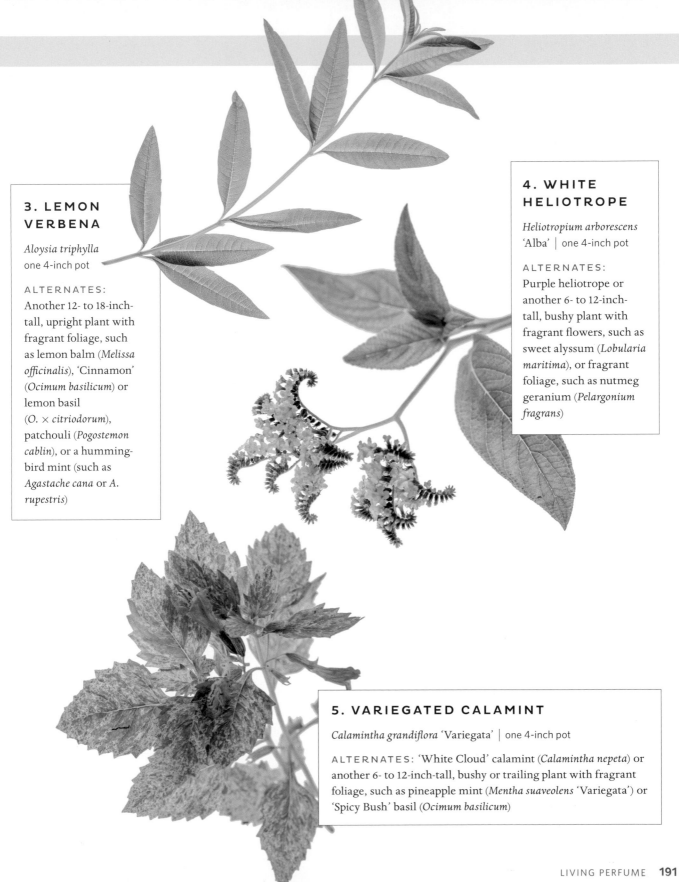

3. LEMON VERBENA

Aloysia triphylla
one 4-inch pot

ALTERNATES:
Another 12- to 18-inch-tall, upright plant with fragrant foliage, such as lemon balm (*Melissa officinalis*), 'Cinnamon' (*Ocimum basilicum*) or lemon basil (*O. × citriodorum*), patchouli (*Pogostemon cablin*), or a humming-bird mint (such as *Agastache cana* or *A. rupestris*)

4. WHITE HELIOTROPE

Heliotropium arborescens 'Alba' | one 4-inch pot

ALTERNATES:
Purple heliotrope or another 6- to 12-inch-tall, bushy plant with fragrant flowers, such as sweet alyssum (*Lobularia maritima*), or fragrant foliage, such as nutmeg geranium (*Pelargonium fragrans*)

5. VARIEGATED CALAMINT

Calamintha grandiflora 'Variegata' | one 4-inch pot

ALTERNATES: 'White Cloud' calamint (*Calamintha nepeta*) or another 6- to 12-inch-tall, bushy or trailing plant with fragrant foliage, such as pineapple mint (*Mentha suaveolens* 'Variegata') or 'Spicy Bush' basil (*Ocimum basilicum*)

LIVING PERFUME
season by season

You'll be immersed in fragrance right from the first day, as you ruffle the foliage when handling the plants: pungent **PLATINUM BLONDE** lavender, citrusy lemon verbena, and sweet-minty variegated calamint. There will also likely be a few early flowers on the white heliotrope, releasing a sweet baby-powder scent.

All five of these plants can tolerate quite a bit of cold, but it's best to wait until temperatures consistently stay above freezing before getting this container started. The jasmine will show off best if you give it some kind of support. For extra stability, put the trellis or tuteur in the container first, then add the potting soil and plants. Water thoroughly once everything is in place.

Don't hesitate to get up close and personal with your scented container planting: gently rub the leaves of the **PLATINUM BLONDE** lavender, lemon verbena, and variegated calamint to release their aromas, and take a good long sniff of the white heliotrope, lavender, and **FIONA SUNRISE** jasmine blossoms. Then step back and take in the beauty of the white heliotrope, light purple lavender, white jasmine, and pink calamint flowers, as well as the showy foliage: bright yellow on the jasmine, gray-green edged with creamy yellow on the lavender, and white-spotted light green on the calamint.

Water when rain is lacking, allowing the top inch or two of potting soil to dry out in between. Apply a liquid fertilizer every 14 days or so, too. As the jasmine stems elongate, gently wrap them around or tie them to the support to encourage vertical growth.

TIDBITS TIPS AND TRICKS

THE RIGHT AMOUNT OF SCENT. It's tempting to pack your pots with all the scented flowers you can find, but it's best to use some restraint. Having more than one or two fragrant plants in bloom at one time in a limited space makes it difficult to appreciate each one; in fact, too much intense scent can be downright unpleasant. Spread out the experience by choosing two or three perfumed bloomers that flower in different seasons or at different times of the day, then fill out the rest of the five with plants that have scented leaves, which will wait until you rub them to release their aromas.

SNIFF FOR YOURSELF. When it comes to container combinations, fragrance is a very subjective feature. Just as with colors, scents can be pleasurable to some people and objectionable to others, so you can't always depend on written descriptions.

MID TO LATE SUMMER

The great thing about fragrant foliage plants is that you can appreciate them any time during the growing season, even when their flowers are finished or not open yet. And when they have colorful foliage — as on **PLATINUM BLONDE** lavender and variegated calamint — so much the better! That's not to say that blooms are lacking in this perfumed planter: the white heliotrope and variegated calamint should still have plenty of flowers now, and you might get a few blooms on the jasmine and lemon verbena.

Regular watering and fertilizing will keep your fragrant planting in peak condition through the dog days. Occasional grooming is important, too: clip off the lavender spikes and heliotrope flower clusters once they drop their blossoms, and remove any dead or damaged leaves. You may also need to trim back some of the jasmine and lemon verbena stems and remove a few shoots of the heliotrope.

FALL

The various scents and colors from late summer continue on into early fall, at least. The shoot tips of **FIONA SUNRISE** jasmine may take on a reddish blush now, too.

Keep up with watering and grooming — but not fertilizing — as long as the planter looks good. In early to mid fall, transplant the variegated calamint to your garden; it's usually winter-hardy as far north as Zone 5. **PLATINUM BLONDE** lavender might be hardy that far north, too, but it has a better chance from a spring planting, so if you want to keep it, pot it up and keep it in a cool, bright place for the winter. Those overwintering conditions will also work for the jasmine, lemon verbena, and heliotrope.

If possible, sniff the plants for yourself before you buy them; that way, you can be sure their scents are appealing and not appalling.

SWEET-SMELLING HERBS. Make the herb section a stop on your shopping expeditions for scented plants. Many herbs offer enticingly aromatic foliage, and they often have pretty flowers as well. Lavenders (*Lavandula*), for instance, are traditional favorites and can grow beautifully in containers. For spicy scents, consider kitchen herbs such as culinary sage (*Salvia officinalis*), upright or trailing rosemary (*Rosmarinus officinalis*), or basils (*Ocimum*). A few with a fruity fragrance include lemon balm (*Melissa officinalis*) and pineapple sage (*Salvia elegans*), as well as the lemon verbena (*Aloysia triphylla*) in this five-plant container. Mints (*Mentha*) are marvelous, too, as are all kinds of scented geraniums (*Pelargonium*), which offer scents ranging from peppermint to citrus to spice to rose.

ASIAN-INSPIRED *Beauty*

CONTAINER COMBINATIONS aren't always about abundant bloom and in-your-face color. Sometimes, you may want to enjoy a sense of quiet and serenity — near your favorite sitting area, for instance, or on a deck or patio where you like to relax in the evening. While you may not be able to replicate many of the traditional features of an Asian-style garden in a container, you *can* use some of them, including a range of soothing greens and a variety of classic Asian plants to create a feeling of soothing tranquility. This set of blue-green glazed pots incorporates those elements with just five plants, including an elegant fern, grasslike and mosslike groundcovers, a muted blue hosta, and a bonsailike feature plant.

PARTIAL SHADE

CONTAINERS: 12" WIDE × 10" HIGH; 9" WIDE × 8" HIGH; 6" WIDE × 5" HIGH

PLANTS:

1 Ming aralia (*Polyscias fruticosa*)

2 Dwarf mondo grass (*Ophiopogon japonicus* 'Nana')

3 Japanese painted fern (*Athyrium niponicum* var. *pictum*)

4 'Dorset Blue' hosta (*Hosta*)

5 Irish moss (*Sagina subulata*)

195

THE 5-PLANT PALETTE

1. MING ARALIA

Polyscias fruticosa │ one 12- to 18-inch-tall plant

ALTERNATES: Another 12- to 24-inch-tall, upright, green-leaved, woody or tropical plant with a treelike form, such as 'Green Waterfall' Japanese maple (*Acer palmatum*); or a relatively compact bamboo, such as *Pleioblastus akebono* or *Sasa veitchii*

3. JAPANESE PAINTED FERN

Athyrium niponicum var. *pictum* │ one 6- to 8-inch pot

ALTERNATES: 'Pewter Lace' Japanese painted fern or 'Ghost' lady fern (*Athyrium*); another green or grayish, arching, 6- to 12-inch-tall fern; or a compact barrenwort (*Epimedium*), such as *E.* × *youngianum*

2. DWARF MONDO GRASS

Ophiopogon japonicus 'Nana' │ five 3- to 4-inch pots

ALTERNATES: 'Gyoku-ryu' mondo grass, or another 1- to 6-inch-tall, spreading plant, such as 'Emerald Chip' ajuga (*Ajuga reptans*), European wild ginger (*Asarum europaeum*), or peacock spikemoss (*Selaginella uncinata*)

4. 'DORSET BLUE' HOSTA

Hosta | one 4- to 6-inch pot

ALTERNATES: 'Baby Bunting', 'Blue Moon', 'Blue Mouse Ears', 'Blue Cadet', 'Fragrant Blue', or another 4- to 6-inch-tall, mounded plant with blue, gray, or silvery leaves, such as 'Callaway' mottled ginger (*Asarum shuttleworthii*) or 'Silver Gem' violet (*Viola walteri*)

5. IRISH MOSS

Sagina subulata | one 6-inch pot

ALTERNATES: Another ground-hugging, creeping plant with rich green leaves, such as creeping wire vine (*Muehlenbeckia axillaris*), baby's tears (*Soleirolia soleirolii*), or Corsican mint (*Mentha requienii*)

ASIAN-INSPIRED BEAUTY
season by season

You'll enjoy this calming combination of greens and blues right from the beginning, thanks to the interplay of interesting leaves as well as the cool colors of the containers themselves. You might also see a few tiny white blooms on the Irish moss.

Many of these plants are quite cold-tolerant, but ming aralia hates getting chilled, so wait until nighttime temperatures are sure to stay above 60°F/15°C before starting your container collection. (Or, plant earlier but keep the pot with the ming aralia and dwarf mondo grass in a bright spot indoors until the weather warms up.) When you're ready to plant the smallest pot, set the hosta in first. Remove the Irish moss from its nursery pot and use garden scissors to cut off the bottom half of the rootball; then cut or gently pull the top growth into four parts and plant them around the hosta.

As the plants fill out, you'll appreciate their various forms and textures: lacy, treelike ming aralia and clump-forming Japanese painted fern; grassy, tufted dwarf mondo grass; mounded, broad-leaved 'Dorset Blue' hosta; and tiny-leaved, ground-hugging Irish moss.

Water regularly so the potting soil doesn't dry out completely (the top ½ to 1 inch is okay), and use a liquid fertilizer every 10 to 14 days.

TIDBITS
TIPS
AND
TRICKS

EXPERIMENTING WITH HOSTAS. Hostas (*Hosta*) are among the best-known and -loved perennials for shady gardens. Once you've explored some of the readily available hybrids, you may want to indulge in some of the newer selections or hard-to-find species. They tend to be more expensive, though, and the plants are often on the small side. Growing these precious gems in a container for a season or two gives you an opportunity to protect and pamper them, so they'll be able to fill out more quickly without getting smothered by bigger companions or falling prey to slugs and other hungry critters.

CHOOSING THE RIGHT BAMBOO. Bamboos are a traditional element of Asian gardens, but the prospect of planting these notorious spreaders in your yard can be daunting — or even illegal, in some areas. Growing them in containers makes it much

The muted greens and blues of these Asian-inspired containers are a welcome sight on hot summer days, enhancing the cool comfort of your favorite shady spot. You may also see some pale lavender to near-white blooms: bell-shaped on the dwarf mondo grass and trumpet-shaped on the 'Dorset Blue' hosta.

Continue watering and fertilizing regularly to keep the plants growing steadily. If you don't want the hosta flowers (some folks like them and some don't), clip off the flowering stems at the base as they appear; otherwise, wait until all of the flowers have dropped to remove them. Trim off any dead or damaged leaves as needed.

This five-plant collection looks lovely into autumn. Eventually, the hosta leaves will turn yellow to brown. Frost will brown the Japanese painted fern foliage, too, but the dwarf mondo grass and Irish moss are evergreen. The ming aralia will keep its leaves, as long as it doesn't get too cold.

Keep watering (but not fertilizing) as long as the plants look good. If you want to keep the ming aralia over winter, bring its pot (with the dwarf mondo grass) indoors before temperatures drop below 60°F/15°C, and keep it in a bright, warm place; otherwise, discard it in your compost pile. Transplant the others to your garden in early fall (dwarf mondo grass is hardy to Zone 6, Irish moss to Zone 5 or 6, Japanese painted fern to Zone 4, and 'Dorset Blue' hosta to Zone 3), or keep them in their pots in a bright and cool but frost-free place for the winter.

easier to control their creeping roots and shows them off to advantage, too, by corralling them into handsome clumps. Just keep in mind that large, vigorously growing kinds can exert a lot of force as their roots expand, eventually breaking or poking through plastic, ceramic, clay, and even thin metal. If you'd like to include a bamboo in your Asian-inspired container collection, consider a smaller-scale running type, such as *Sasa veitchii*, and be sure to keep the container on a solid surface, such as a deck or paved area, so the roots can't creep out of the drainage holes and into the soil. Or, choose a naturally clump-forming kind, such as fountain bamboo (*Fargesia nitida*) or umbrella bamboo (*F. murielae*).

ANNUAL *Appeal*

ANNUALS ARE AMONG THE MOST POPULAR choices for filling pots and planters because they flower abundantly over a long period, come in an amazing array of colors, shapes, and sizes, and are widely available. They last only one growing season, but they're relatively inexpensive, which means that you have the opportunity to experiment with new colors and combinations to give your favorite containers a different look each year. This tapered, round resin planter holds a variety of flowering and foliage annuals, in shades of yellow and white to complement the container's terra-cotta color.

FULL SUN TO PARTIAL SHADE

CONTAINER: 12" WIDE × 12" HIGH

PLANTS:

1. BANDANA WHITE lantana (*Lantana camara* 'Ban Whit')
2. 'ColorBlaze LifeLime' coleus (*Solenostemon scutellarioides*)
3. DIAMOND FROST spurge (*Euphorbia hypericifolia* 'Inneuphe')
4. 'Sundew Springs' loosestrife (*Lysimachia*)
5. SUPERBELLS LEMON SLICE calibrachoa (*Calibrachoa* 'Uscal5302m')

1. BANDANA WHITE LANTANA

Lantana camara 'Ban Whit' │ one 3- to 4-inch pot

ALTERNATES: **BANDANA LEMON ZEST** ('Bani Yelbic')
or **LUSCIOUS PIÑA COLADA** ('Lanz0004') lantana or
another 8- to 12-inch-tall, bushy annual with white or yellow-
and-white flowers, such as 'Buddy White' globe amaranth
(*Gomphrena globosa*) or 'Graffiti White' starflower (*Pentas lanceolata*)

2. 'COLORBLAZE LIFELIME' COLEUS

Solenostemon scutellarioides
one 3- to 4-inch pot

ALTERNATES: 'Fairway
Yellow' or 'Lime Frills'
coleus or another 8- to
14-inch-tall, upright annual
with yellow or yellow-
and-white leaves, such as
'True Yellow' Joseph's coat
(*Alternanthera ficoidea*)

3. DIAMOND FROST **SPURGE**

Euphorbia hypericifolia 'Inneuphe' | one 3- to 4-inch pot

ALTERNATES: **BREATHLESS WHITE** ('Balbrewite')
spurge or another 6- to 12-inch-tall, bushy or trailing annual
with white flowers, such as 'Bombay White' fanflower
(*Scaevola aemula*) or 'Serena White' angelonia (*Angelonia
angustifolia*)

4. 'SUNDEW SPRINGS' LOOSESTRIFE

Lysimachia | one 3- to 4-inch pot

ALTERNATES: 'Walkabout Sunset' dense-flowered
loosestrife (*Lysimachia congestiflora*) or another 2- to 4-inch-
tall, trailing annual with yellow or yellow-and-green
leaves or yellow flowers, such as **GOLD DUST** mecardonia
(*Mecardonia* 'Usmeca8205') or **SUNBINI** creeping zinnia
(*Sanvitalia* 'Starbini Superbini')

5. SUPERBELLS LEMON SLICE **CALIBRACHOA**

Calibrachoa 'Uscal5302m'
one 3- to 4-inch pot

ALTERNATES:
Another 6- to 8-inch-
tall, mounded or
trailing annual with
yellow flowers, such
as 'Moonlight' nas-
turtium (*Tropaeolum
majus*), 'Sundial Yellow'
purslane (*Portulaca
grandiflora*), or **YELLOW
CHARM** bidens (*Bidens
ferulifolia* 'Danyel9')

ANNUAL APPEAL

season by season

The bright yellow leaves of the 'ColorBlaze LifeLime' coleus and 'Sundew Springs' loosestrife provide cheery color right from the start, accented with the first few blooms on the **BANDANA WHITE** lantana, **DIAMOND FROST** spurge, and **SUPERBELLS LEMON SLICE** calibrachoa.

Don't be in too much of a hurry to get this container started, because some of these annuals (especially the coleus) don't like to get chilled. It's best to wait until nighttime temperatures are sure to stay above 55°F/13°C. After planting, water thoroughly to settle the potting soil around the roots.

You start getting the full effect of the color theme now, when the yellow 'ColorBlaze LifeLime' coleus and 'Sundew Springs' loosestrife leaves are joined by the **BANDANA WHITE** lantana, with creamy yellow-to-white clusters; **DIAMOND FROST** spurge, with lacy white blooms; and **SUPERBELLS LEMON SLICE** calibrachoa, with bright yellow-and-white blossoms. The loosestrife also chimes in with clustered, bright yellow blooms by midsummer.

There's not much to do now, other than watering (letting the top inch or so of potting soil dry out in between) and applying a liquid fertilizer every 7 to 10 days.

TIDBITS TIPS AND TRICKS

ANNUAL OR TENDER PERENNIAL? It's interesting to note that many common container annuals aren't actually "true" annuals — plants that sprout from seed, grow, flower, and set seed within one growing season, such as zinnias (*Zinnia*) and marigolds (*Tagetes*). Instead, they are often tender perennials that just get treated like annuals. Tender perennials, such as the five plants in this colorful combination, are able to live from year to year in warm to hot climates (or if you bring them indoors for the winter), but they grow quickly enough and flower so freely that you can buy new ones each year and toss them in your compost pile at the end of the season. Both kinds of plants work out equally well for one-year displays, with one difference: true annuals usually bloom best if you keep the finished flowers clipped off (a process called deadheading), so they put their energy into forming new blossoms instead of seeds. Regular deadheading also helps to keep tender perennials looking nice, but it usually isn't as important with them as with true annuals.

This container continues to look lovely all through the summer, thanks to the cheery combination of white, yellow, and cream-colored flowers and foliage.

Keep up with watering and fertilizing now to support all of those beautiful flowers and lush leaves. Most of the blooming plants in this container will neatly drop their finished blossoms, so you don't need to bother much with deadheading: simply sweep up those that are on the ground. Pinch off any flower buds that form on the tips of the coleus stems, and trim any overly long stems on any of the plants to keep them all in proportion to each other and to the container.

The color just keeps coming with this annual-filled planter. The 'Sundew Springs' loosestrife is usually finished flowering by early fall, but its foliage — as well as that of the 'ColorBlaze LifeLime' coleus — continues to look good until frost, as do the various flowers.

Maintain the watering routine as long as the plants look good. Covering the container with a sheet at night can help it get through a light early frost, but eventually cold will call a halt to the growing season; at that point, pull out all of the plants and add them to your compost pile.

THE BENEFITS OF MULTI-PACKS. Individually potted annuals are handy for container plantings, since you usually need only one of each kind for a five-plant container. But if you can find the same ones in packs of four or six plants, consider giving them a try. The individual plants will be smaller at first, but they'll usually catch up quickly with regular watering and fertilizing in a container. Pot up the leftovers individually for spots of color in other places, or use them as fillers in your flower beds to complement your container combinations.

COLOR SMARTS. When you're shopping for container annuals in spring, it's tempting to load up on those that are filled with flowers, such as blue lobelia (*Lobelia erinus*), pansies and violas (*Viola*), sweet alyssum (*Lobularia maritima*), and twinspurs (*Diascia*). These cool-season annuals are a delight for early color, but they often fizzle out when summer heat arrives, leaving you with sad-looking containers by July. Go ahead and enjoy them, if you want, but to have colorful pots and planters from midsummer into fall, too, plan on replacing them with heat-loving annuals in early summer.

PERENNIAL PUNCH *for* SHADE

IF YOU'RE LOOKING FOR SOMETHING different to fill your pots and planters, consider bringing some hardy perennials into the mix. While it's true that perennials typically don't flower as long as common container annuals, some offer interesting leaf textures and colors that rival the brightest blooms for visual impact. Perennials may also have other interesting features, such as attractive seed heads or showy fall color, to add seasonal variety. They also tend to be available in larger sizes than most annuals, making them ideal for filling sizable containers quickly. This cubic, black patio planter features a five-plant collection of dependable perennials to brighten a shady site with both foliage and flowers.

PARTIAL TO FULL SHADE

CONTAINER: 18" LONG × 18" WIDE × 18" HIGH

PLANTS:

1 Autumn fern (*Dryopteris erythrosora*)

2 PENNY'S PINK hellebore (*Helleborus* 'Abcrd01')

3 'Sunrise Falls' foamy bells (×*Heucherella*)

4 Chinese wild ginger (*Asarum splendens*)

5 'White Nancy' spotted deadnettle (*Lamium maculatum*)

2. PENNY'S PINK HELLEBORE

Helleborus 'Abcrd01'
one 6-inch pot

ALTERNATES:
'Ivory Prince' hellebore
or another 8- to 18-inch-
tall, mounded or upright
perennial with green, blue,
or variegated leaves, such
as 'June' or 'Tokudama
Aureonebulosa' hosta
(*Hosta*), 'Gilt Edge' toad
lily (*Tricyrtis formosana*),
or hardy begonia (*Begonia
grandis*)

1. AUTUMN FERN

Dryopteris erythrosora
one 6-inch pot

ALTERNATES: Another
upright to arching fern,
such as Christmas fern
(*Polystichum acrostichoides*)
or a lady fern (*Athyrium*),
or another 10- to 18-inch-
tall, lacy-leaved perennial,
such as 'Deutschland' or
'Visions in Pink' astilbe
(*Astilbe*)

3. 'SUNRISE FALLS' FOAMY BELLS

× *Heucherella* | one 6-inch pot

ALTERNATES: 'Gold Zebra' or 'Stoplight' foamy bells
or another 6- to 8-inch-tall, mounded, arching, or trailing perennial with yellow foliage, such as 'Citronelle' or
'Pistache' heuchera (*Heuchera*) or 'All Gold' Hakone grass
(*Hakonechloa macra*)

4. CHINESE WILD GINGER

Asarum splendens │ one 6-inch pot

ALTERNATES: European wild ginger (*Asarum europaeum*) or another 4- to 8-inch-tall, mounded perennial with rounded to heart-shaped, green or green-and-silver leaves, such as a bergenia (*Bergenia*) or 'Dark Vader' or 'Milky Way' lungwort (*Pulmonaria*)

5. 'WHITE NANCY' SPOTTED DEADNETTLE

Lamium maculatum │ one 4-inch pot

ALTERNATES: **PINK CHABLIS** spotted deadnettle (*Lamium maculatum* 'Checkin') or another 4- to 6-inch-tall, arching or trailing perennial with green, silvery, or variegated leaves, such as sweet woodruff (*Galium odoratum*), pineapple mint (*Mentha suaveolens* 'Variegata'), or variegated mondo grass (*Ophiopogon japonicus* 'Variegatus')

PERENNIAL PUNCH FOR SHADE
season by season

SPRING

This five-plant perennial partnership looks great right from day one, thanks to the variety of leaf sizes, shapes, and colors. The foliage of 'Sunrise Falls' foamy bells tends to grab your eye first: it's mostly bright yellow, which picks up the yellow veining in the **PENNY'S PINK** hellebore leaves, but it also has orangey red markings that echo the orange new fronds of the autumn fern. And in the center, the leaves of Chinese wild ginger include both the deep green of the hellebore leaves and the silver of the 'White Nancy' spotted deadnettle. The clustered white flowers of the deadnettle and the bowl-shaped, dusky pink blooms of the hellebore are a delightful complement to all that leafy goodness.

All of these perennials are quite cold-tolerant, so you can get this container started as soon as you have all of the plants, as long as they're acclimated to the outdoors.

EARLY TO MID SUMMER

The fabulous foliage features from spring continue into summer, with a few changes: as the weather warms, the orange new fronds of autumn fern mature to a glossy green, and the older leaves of 'Sunrise Falls' foamy bells tend to turn solid yellow, though the new leaves still show some of the orangey red veining. 'White Nancy' spotted deadnettle is still flowering, and the foamy bells begins blooming in earnest, with loose, spiky clusters of small but abundant white flowers.

Water when rain is lacking to keep the potting soil evenly moist (but not soggy), and apply a liquid fertilizer every 10 to 14 days. Clip off the finished flowers of the hellebore, as well as any dead or damaged leaves on any of the plants.

TIDBITS TIPS AND TRICKS

TERRIFIC TRAILING PERENNIALS. The usual route for choosing plants for containers is to have one or more upright shapes, one or more bushy shapes, and one or two trailing plants. When you're working with perennials, it's easy to find upright and bushy forms, but trailing ones may not be as obvious. The trick here is to look among plants usually considered as ground covers. Some creeping or cascading perennials with pretty flowers and/or handsome leaves include silvery spotted deadnettle (*Lamium maculatum*), mints (*Mentha*), creeping foamflowers (*Tiarella*), and ajugas (*Ajuga*) for shade, and hardy geraniums (*Geranium*), ice plants (*Delosperma*), and creeping sedums (*Sedum*) and thymes (*Thymus*) for sun.

PERENNIALS FOR SUN. For sunny sites, look for perennials with long flowering seasons, such as blanket flowers (*Gaillardia*) and coreopsis (*Coreopsis*). If you regularly

MID TO LATE SUMMER

Lovely leaf colors and textures are still the highlight of this container, with the bonus of dainty white blooms continuing to appear on 'Sunrise Falls' foamy bells. You'll also see interesting patterns of dark dots appearing on the backs of the older autumn fern fronds; they are the spore cases (the fern equivalent of seed heads in flowering plants).

Continue to water whenever rain is lacking, and keep fertilizing until late summer. Regular grooming will help to keep the container looking its very best: Remove any dead or discolored foliage, and cut off the finished flower spikes of the foamy bells at their base. Trim off some of the older fronds of the fern, too, as well as some of the trailing stems of the dead-nettle and foamy bells, to keep them in proportion to the other plants and to the container.

FALL

These pretty perennials will continue to brighten any shady space through most or all of the autumn months, thanks to the handsome, long-lasting leaves. The 'Sunrise Falls' foamy bells may be even more striking now, as cooler weather tends to bring out more of the reddish leaf markings, and it may continue to produce new flowers, too.

Keep watering as long as the plants are still growing. At the end of the growing season, you have several options: you could transplant the perennials to your garden if they are winter-hardy in your area (in this collection, the ginger should be hardy to Zone 6, the autumn fern and hellebore to Zone 5, the foamy bells to Zone 4, and the deadnettle to Zone 3); you could leave them in their container and move the container into a sheltered place, such as an unheated garage or cool basement, in mid to late fall; or, you could leave the whole thing outside and hope for the best, if the plants are hardy to at least one zone colder than yours.

clip off the faded blossoms, they can bloom for many weeks, or even months. Those with interesting forms and foliage textures, such as sedums and other succulents, and ornamental grasses, such as Mexican feather grass (*Stipa tenuissima*) and fountain grasses (*Pennisetum*), are also super for catching the eye even when they're not in bloom.

GOOD FOR THE BUDGET. Perennial-based combinations are a great investment, because you're not tossing them into your compost pile at the end of each growing season. You can buy small, relatively inexpensive starter plants, enjoy them in pots or planters, and then transplant them to a bed or border. It works the other way, too: if you have extra pieces left when you divide established perennials in spring, they can make great fillers in your containers.

TROPICAL
Sunset

NO MATTER WHERE YOU LIVE, CONTAINERS packed with bright blooms and lush leaves can bring a touch of the tropics to any part of your outdoor living space. True tropicals, however, tend to be very tolerant of heat and humidity, so they're particularly choice for areas with sultry summers. Many can get very large, so they're an excellent choice for making a spectacular show in sizable pots on a patio or by a pool. Not quite ready for a tropical profusion of brilliant reds, hot pinks, bright yellow, and bold orange? This rust-colored resin beehive planter features a five-plant grouping of colorful leaves accented with warm-hued flowers in a sunset-shaded palette.

FULL SUN

CONTAINER: 20" WIDE × 18" HIGH

PLANTS:

1 'Tropical Yellow' canna (*Canna*)

2 Caribbean copper plant (*Euphorbia cotinifolia*)

3 'Caribbean Sunset' Mexican heather (*Cuphea cyanea*)

4 'Rustic Orange' coleus (*Solenostemon scutellarioides*)

5 'Sweet Georgia Heart Light Green' sweet potato vine (*Ipomoea batatas*)

1. 'TROPICAL YELLOW' CANNA

Canna
one 4- to 6-inch pot

ALTERNATES:
'Tangelo', 'Yellow Futurity', or another compact, yellow- or orange-flowered canna, or another 18- to 36-inch-tall tropical plant with yellow-variegated foliage, such as 'Dancing Flame' scarlet sage (*Salvia splendens*) or variegated shell ginger (*Alpinia zerumbet* 'Variegata')

2. CARIBBEAN COPPER PLANT

Euphorbia cotinifolia | one 4- to 6-inch pot

ALTERNATES: Another bushy, 2- to 4-foot-tall tropical plant with colorful leaves, such as a copperleaf (*Acalypha wilkesiana*) or 'Red Heart' or 'Variegated Heart' bloodleaf (*Iresine herbstii*)

4. 'RUSTIC ORANGE' COLEUS

Solenostemon scutellarioides
one 4-inch pot

ALTERNATES:
Another 12- to
18-inch-tall,
orangey or
yellow-leaved
coleus, such
as 'ColorBlaze
Keystone Kopper',
'ColorBlaze
Sedona', or
'ColorBlaze
LifeLime'

3. 'CARIBBEAN SUNSET' MEXICAN HEATHER

Cuphea cyanea
one 4-inch pot

ALTERNATES:
'David Verity' or
'Strybing Sunset' cuphea
(*Cuphea*), or another
12- to 24-inch-tall, bushy
tropical plant with
orange or red flowers,
such as a Sun Harmony
or SunPatiens Series
impatiens (*Impatiens*)

5. 'SWEET GEORGIA HEART LIGHT GREEN' SWEET POTATO VINE

Ipomoea batatas | one 4-inch pot

ALTERNATES: 'Bright Ideas Lime', 'Sweet Caroline Light
Green', or another yellow-leaved sweet potato vine, or
another trailing, yellow-variegated plant such as variegated
potato vine (*Solanum jasminoides* 'Variegatum')

TROPICAL SUNSET

season by season

SPRING

Wait until the weather has warmed up — with nighttime temperatures at least 55°F/13°C — before getting this heat-loving container collection started. Water after planting to settle the plants into the potting soil. Wash your hands after handling the Caribbean copper plant to remove any of the irritating sap the plant releases if you damage its leaves or stems.

Though the pot might look a little sparse at first, you'll get a taste of the display to come right from the beginning, thanks to the colorful foliage: deep red Caribbean copper plant, gold-edged orange on 'Rustic Orange' coleus, and bright yellow on 'Sweet Georgia Heart Light Green' sweet potato vine. There may also be a few early, orange blooms on the 'Caribbean Sunset' Mexican heather.

EARLY TO MID SUMMER

As your tropical combination fills out, the foreground plants are most obvious at first, with 'Caribbean Sunset' Mexican heather, 'Rustic Orange' coleus, and 'Sweet Georgia Heart Light Green' sweet potato vine creating a harmony of oranges and yellows, complemented by the rich green of the 'Tropical Yellow' canna leaves. You'll also see a touch of burgundy from the Caribbean copper plant, echoing the dark stems of the Mexican heather.

Let the top inch or so of potting soil dry out between waterings, and apply a liquid fertilizer every 10 to 14 days. Other than that, there's nothing to do but watch your tropicals jump into luxuriant growth.

TIDBITS TIPS AND TRICKS

TIMING FOR TROPICALS. Tropical plants are ideal if you tend to get a late start on your container plantings. They tend to sulk if they get chilled, so planting them early may actually set back your display by a few weeks. Wait until the weather is dependably warm both day and night — ideally 60°F/15°C or higher for most tropicals, even if that's not until early summer — and they'll jump into growth and fill out quickly. If you're eager to get your containers filled with color before then, plant them up in early to mid spring with potted bulbs and cool-season annuals, such as pansies and violas (*Viola*), forget-me-nots (*Myosotis sylvatica*), sweet alyssum (*Lobularia maritima*), and blue lobelia (*Lobelia erinus*). Enjoy them into early summer, then pull them out once the weather's warm and it's time for your tropicals.

The dog days bring out the best in these heat-lovers, filling out the planter with a bounty of color. It'll take a lot of water to support these thriving tropicals, so check the container frequently and water thoroughly and often when rain is lacking. (That may mean every day in hot, dry spells.) Fertilize more frequently now, too: every 7 to 10 days through the rest of the summer. Remove any dead or damaged leaves regularly, and clip or pinch off developing flower spikes on the coleus. Cut off the canna's flower clusters as they finish, cutting just above the next cluster or leaf lower down on the stem. You'll probably need to cut the sweet potato vine back by a third to a half a time or two during this period, to keep it in proportion to the rest of the plants. Avoid cutting or breaking the Caribbean copper plant leaves or stems whenever possible, because they will release a sticky white sap that can be irritating to skin and eyes and toxic if ingested.

This five-plant combination keeps looking better and better into early fall, as long as the weather stays on the warm side, and will remain attractive until nights start dipping into the chilly range.

Continue to water as long as the plants are growing. Draping the entire grouping with a sheet at night may help it get through an early frost or two, but eventually the plants will begin dropping their leaves. It's usually easiest to treat the coleus, Mexican heather, and sweet potato vine as annuals. You could do the same with the canna and Caribbean copper plant, too, and just compost everything. (Wear gloves when handling the Caribbean copper plant to protect your hands from the irritating sap.) Or, cut off the top growth of the canna, coleus, Mexican heather, and sweet potato vine, haul the whole container into a cool but frost-free place for the winter, and water just enough to keep the potting soil from drying out completely.

TROPICALS FOR SHADE. No sun? No problem! There are plenty of top-notch tropicals with fabulous foliage that can give a lush look to partial- to full-shade containers. Some of the easiest-to-find options include broad-leaved caladiums (*Caladium*), spiky dracaenas (*Dracaena*), and loads of coleus (*Solenostemon scutellarioides*) and fancy-leaved begonias (*Begonia*), but those are just the beginning. For something different, look for sanchezia (*Sanchezia speciosa*), with green leaves that are veined with yellow, or 'Triostar' stromanthe (*Stromanthe sanguinea*), with cream- to white-and-green with deep pink undersides. You can find many other terrific foliage tropicals for summer containers in the houseplant section at your favorite greenhouse or garden center.

Lovely LEAVES

FLOWERS HAVE LONG BEEN THE FOCUS of container plantings, but these days, you can create amazing combinations based on foliage alone. Choose a variety of plant shapes and leaf textures in just one or two colors, like green or silver, for an effect of subtle sophistication. Or, go for a high-impact collection of brightly colored and patterned leaves for a container that's guaranteed to attract attention. Foliage-based pots like this one work well in any growing conditions, but they're particularly useful in shady sites, because they can supply a long season of color where there's not enough light to support abundant blooming. This rectangular resin planter holds a variety of upright, bushy, and trailing beauties to grace a site with morning sun and afternoon shade or light, all-day shade.

PARTIAL SHADE

CONTAINER: 24" LONG × 12" WIDE × 12" DEEP

PLANTS:

1 Croton (*Codiaeum variegatum* var. *pictum*)

2 'Pacific Crest' foamflower (*Tiarella*)

3 'Redmond' rex begonia (*Begonia rex*)

4 'Under the Sea Bone Fish' coleus (*Solenostemon scutellarioides*)

5 'Variegated Heart' bloodleaf (*Iresine herbstii*)

1. CROTON

Codiaeum variegatum
var. *pictum*
one 4- to 6-inch pot

ALTERNATES:
Another 8- to 18-inch-
tall, mounded to upright
plant with broad or
slender, colorful leaves,
such as 'Banana Boat'
broadleaf sedge (*Carex
siderosticha*), 'ColorBlaze
Sedona' coleus
(*Solenostemon
scutellarioides*), or
'Electra' heuchera
(*Heuchera*)

2. 'PACIFIC CREST' FOAMFLOWER

Tiarella | one 4- to 6-inch pot

ALTERNATES: 'Jeepers Creepers' foamflower or another
4- to 6-inch-tall, mounded or trailing plant with jagged
or rounded, colorful leaves, such as 'Gold Zebra' or 'Solar
Eclipse' foamy bells (×*Heucherella*) or 'Troy's Gold' spur-
flower (*Plectranthus ciliata*)

3. 'REDMOND' REX BEGONIA

Begonia rex
one 4- to 6-inch pot

ALTERNATES:
'Harmony's Red
Robin' or 'Miami
Storm' rex begonia or
another 6- to 12-inch-
tall, mounded plant
with broad, colorful
leaves, such as 'Florida
Cardinal' or 'Red
Ruffles' caladium
(*Caladium*) or 'Autumn
Leaves' or 'Fire Chief'
heuchera (*Heuchera*)

4. 'UNDER THE SEA BONE FISH' COLEUS

Solenostemon scutellarioides │ one 4 to 6-inch pot

ALTERNATES: 'Colissima Raspberry', 'India Frills', or 'Kiwi Fern' coleus, or another 6- to 10-inch-tall, mounded or trailing plant with jagged or ferny, colorful leaves, such as 'Burgundy Lace' Japanese painted fern (*Athyrium niponicum* var. *pictum*) or RITA'S GOLD Boston fern (*Nephrolepis exaltata* 'Aurea')

5. 'VARIEGATED HEART' BLOODLEAF

Iresine herbstii │ one 4- to 6-inch pot

ALTERNATES: Another 12- to 18-inch-tall, upright plant with rounded or grassy, colorful leaves, such as golden Hakone grass (*Hakonechloa macra* 'Aureola'), chameleon plant (*Houttuynia cordata* 'Chameleon'), or leopard plant (*Farfugium japonicum* 'Aureomaculatum')

LOVELY LEAVES

season by season

There's no waiting when it comes to foliage-focused container plantings: the lovely leaves look great from the very first day you put them together. This collection is based on contrasting broad and jagged leaves, primarily in shades of pinkish red, yellow, and green. You might also see some white flowers on the 'Pacific Crest' foamflower now.

Of these five plants, the croton and the rex begonia are the most sensitive to cold. Wait until nighttime temperatures are consistently at least 60°F/15°C before planting, even if that's not until very late spring; you'll lose any advantage of an earlier start if the plants get stunted or drop their leaves due to a chill. Water after planting. Clip off any bloom spikes on the foamflower once they drop their blossoms (or when they appear, if you want to stay with just foliage).

As the days heat up, so does this container collection, with lots of leafy growth. The contrasting plant forms and leaf shapes are still very apparent, but you'll also notice a lot of subtle echoes that visually tie the plants together, including the deep purple center stars in the 'Redmond' rex begonia and 'Pacific Crest' foamflower, the brighter purplish red in the rex begonia and the 'Under the Sea Bone Fish' coleus, the yellow in the 'Variegated Heart' bloodleaf and the croton, and the bright green in the bloodleaf, coleus, and foamflower. There might also be a few scattered, white flowers on the 'Pacific Crest' foamflower through the summer.

Water regularly when rain is lacking to keep the soil moist (though not soggy), and apply a liquid fertilizer every 10 to 14 days. Remove any foamflower bloom spikes, either before the buds open or when they are finished.

TIDBITS TIPS AND TRICKS

MORE FOLIAGE FOR SHADE. When it's time to find foliage plants for shady containers, look beyond the usual annual displays at your favorite local greenhouse or garden center. The houseplants section yields lots of fabulous finds that you can use in outdoor containers in summer and then bring indoors for the winter. Be sure to check out the shade perennials section, too. Hostas (*Hosta*), heucheras (*Heuchera*), foamy bells (×*Heucherella*), a wide variety of ferns, and many other eye-catching hardy perennials adapt readily to life in a container. Transplant them to your garden at the end of the growing season, then dig them up again in the spring for next year's containers or leave them in place to fill your shady beds with color and texture.

LEAFY PLANTS FOR SUNNY SPOTS. There are lots of amazing leafy plants for sunny spaces as well. Among the annuals and tender perennials, look for container favorites such as sweet potato vines (*Ipomoea batatas*), bananas (*Musa*), cannas

The intricate interplay of colors, shapes, and textures keeps your shady foliage container looking fantastic even through the hottest part of the summer.

Keep up with watering and fertilizing through the rest of the summer. A bit of regular grooming will keep the combination looking its very best. Remove any dead, damaged, or discolored leaves, and pinch off any flower buds that form at the tops of the coleus shoots. Also trim back the longest stems of the coleus, bloodleaf, and foamflower by a third to a half to keep all of the plants in proportion to each other and to the container.

You'll enjoy your fabulous foliage container into early autumn, as the plants continue to thrive until temperatures start to dip into the 50s at night.

If you'd like to keep the plants for next year, dismantle the planting in early fall. Transplant the foamflower to your garden (it's usually winter-hardy as far north as Zone 4). Take cuttings of the coleus and bloodleaf, and pot up the begonia and croton; keep them all in a warm, bright place and enjoy them as winter houseplants, then move them back outside when the weather warms again next year.

(*Canna*), purple heart (*Setcreasea pallida*), alternantheras (*Alternanthera*), and sun-tolerant coleus (*Solenostemon scutellarioides*). Then, mix things up with some ornamental grasses, such as fountain grasses (*Pennisetum*) and Japanese blood grass (*Imperata cylindrica* 'Rubra'), and colorful edibles, like 'Bright Lights' Swiss chard (*Beta vulgaris* Cicla Group), 'Redbor' kale (*Brassica oleracea* Acephala Group), variegated or purple basils (*Ocimum*), and 'Bull's Blood' beet (*Beta vulgaris* Conditiva Group).

PRIME SETTINGS FOR FOLIAGE. Flower-filled containers are lovely to look at, but when they're buzzing with bees, most folks are leery of getting too close. For that reason, foliage-based combinations are often a better choice next to benches, steps, doorways, walkways, and other high-traffic areas. Granted, some plants with stunning leaves also produce blooms, but the flowers are secondary; keep them cut off, if you wish, and you'll still have a spectacular container display.

TERRA-COTTA *Charm*

THE CLASSIC CLAY (TERRA-COTTA) POT is the go-to container choice for many gardeners, and for good reasons. The natural colors of clay pots — ranging from bright orange to pinky orange to earthy brown — look great with many plants, and you can find them in shapes to suit any style, from traditional to contemporary. Clay pots come in a wide range of prices, too. Those that have relatively thin sides tend to be less expensive and lighter in weight but are more prone to chipping or cracking. Higher-quality clay containers tend to be heavier and more durable, with thicker sides that do a great job insulating tender roots from heat and cold.

FULL SUN TO PARTIAL SHADE

CONTAINER: 15" WIDE × 13" HIGH

PLANTS:

1 'Lemon Spritzer' cape fuchsia (*Phygelius × rectus*)

2 'Abbey Road' coleus (*Solenostemon scutellarioides*)

3 'Ascot Rainbow' spurge (*Euphorbia × martinii*)

4 'Bright Lights Camouflage' sweet potato vine (*Ipomoea batatas*)

5 'Christa' heuchera (*Heuchera*)

1. 'LEMON SPRITZER' CAPE FUCHSIA

Phygelius × rectus
one 4- to 6-inch pot

ALTERNATES: 'Sunshine' cape fuchsia or another 8- to 18-inch-tall, bushy or spiky plant with yellow-variegated or solid yellow foliage, such as variegated flowering maple (*Abutilon pictum* 'Thompsonii') or 'French Lace' geranium (*Pelargonium crispum*), or yellow flowers, such as 'Summer Glow' hummingbird mint (*Agastache*) or 'Golden Girl' autumn sage (*Salvia*)

2. 'ABBEY ROAD' COLEUS

Solenostemon scutellarioides | one 4-inch pot

ALTERNATES: 'Fishnet Stockings', 'Inky Fingers', 'Dark Star', or another purple-and-green or solid purple coleus, or another 8- to 12-inch-tall, bushy plant with foliage in that color range, such as 'Little Ruby' alternanthera (*Alternanthera dentata*) or purple false eranthemum (*Pseuderanthemum atropurpureum*)

3. 'ASCOT RAINBOW' SPURGE

Euphorbia × martinii | one 4-inch pot

ALTERNATES: Another 6- to 8-inch-tall, bushy plant with small, yellow-and-green or -peach foliage, such as **PLATINUM BLONDE** lavender (*Lavandula angustifolia* 'Momparler') or 'Copper Glow' or 'Sunset Gold' oxalis (*Oxalis vulcanicola*)

4. 'BRIGHT LIGHTS CAMOUFLAGE' SWEET POTATO VINE

Ipomoea batatas | one 4-inch pot

ALTERNATES: 'Sweet Caroline Purple' or another dark-leaved sweet potato vine, or another 4- to 6-inch-tall, mounded or trailing plant with dark foliage, such as 'Purple Lady' bloodleaf (*Iresine herbstii*) or 'Red Threads' Joseph's coat (*Alternanthera ficoidea*)

5. 'CHRISTA' HEUCHERA

Heuchera
one 4- or 6-inch pot

ALTERNATES: 'Midas Touch', 'Peach Flambe', or another peach-colored heuchera, or another 4- to 8-inch-tall, mounded or trailing plant with peach-colored flowers, such as 'Tip Top Apricot' nasturtium (*Tropaeolum majus*) or 'Noa Peach' calibrachoa (*Calibrachoa*)

TERRA-COTTA CHARM

season by season

SPRING

If you like your containers to have instant impact, you'll love this five-plant grouping of fabulous foliage plants. 'Lemon Spritzer' cape fuchsia, with its green-speckled, bright yellow leaves, vies for first impact with the whorled shoots of yellow-edged, gray-green foliage of 'Ascot Rainbow' spurge. The newer growth of the spurge is heavily blushed with coppery pink at this time of year, echoing the peachy colors of the 'Christa' heuchera, as well as the terra-cotta of the container itself. The mottled purple-and-green leaves of 'Abbey Road' coleus and 'Bright Lights Camouflage' sweet potato vine add a touch of darkness that lets the brighter leaves really stand out.

Buy the plants as you find them, but wait until nighttime temperatures stay above 50°F/10°C, because the coleus and sweet potato vine may get stunted if exposed to chilly temperatures. It's a good idea to soak the empty container in a tub of water overnight, so the clay can absorb plenty of water and won't immediately start drawing moisture out of the potting soil once you plant.

EARLY TO MID SUMMER

As the weather gets warmer, the foliage colors and textures of this clay container stay pretty much the same, with the added bonus of dangling, coral-red, yellow-centered trumpets on the 'Lemon Spritzer' cape fuchsia. 'Ascot Rainbow' spurge might bloom now, too, with sprays of chartreuse flowers, but it's not likely to on a relatively small, young plant. The same goes for the 'Christa' heuchera: it might flower now, with loose spikes of tiny, pinkish flowers, or it might not.

The leaves of all of these plants are so beautiful that you probably won't care if any of them bloom, anyway. In fact, you may choose to clip off any flowers that do develop so you can more easily admire the foliage. Otherwise, all you need to do is water regularly to keep the potting soil evenly moist, and add a dose of liquid fertilizer every 10 to 14 days.

TIDBITS TIPS AND TRICKS

WINTER PROTECTION FOR CLAY. Clay is a porous material, which makes it good for plants because it allows a good exchange of moisture and air for their roots. That's a problem in winter, though, when the moisture in the clay expands as it freezes and causes the sides to crack or crumble. To prevent this damage, empty your clay pots in fall and bring them into a sheltered spot (such as a shed or garage) before freezing weather. If that's not practical, look for clay pots that are described as "frost-resistant"; they may eventually crack but should make it through a few winters. (Coating all sides with a clear sealant before planting can provide an extra level of protection.) Or, invest in top-quality "frost-proof" clay containers; they're expensive, but the best can last for many years outdoors with no special treatment.

The various leaf colors and patterns continue to brighten this clay pot through the rest of the summer, with just a few small changes: the 'Ascot Rainbow' spurge will likely lose some or all of its pinkish blush during hot weather, while 'Christa' heuchera tends to appear more pale orange to tan. The 'Lemon Spritzer' cape fuchsia will likely still have some flowers through midsummer, and so might the heuchera. 'Abbey Road' coleus will start producing flower spikes at the shoot tips, but the purplish blooms don't add much interest.

Clip off any flower stalks as they finish — or as they emerge, if you'd rather have just the fabulous foliage, particularly on the coleus. Clip out individual leaves or whole shoots as needed to keep all of the plants in proportion to one another. Plantings growing in clay containers can dry out quickly during hot, dry weather, so pay extra-careful attention to watering now. Continue to use liquid fertilizer every 10 to 14 days.

These lovely leaves continue to look good through early fall, at least: even until cold temperatures nip the coleus and sweet potato vine.

Keep watering and grooming your clay-potted planting as long as it's still growing. Once nights start dipping into the frosty range, it's time to dismantle the planting. Transplant the heuchera to your garden (it should overwinter all right from a fall planting in Zone 5 and south, especially if you protect it with some mulch). If you want to keep the cape fuchsia and spurge, it's best to pot them up and keep them in a cool, bright spot for the winter. Discard the coleus and sweet potato vine in your compost pile unless you want to keep them as houseplants in a warm, bright place for the winter.

CLEANING CLAY POTS. Over time, the bright, uniform color of new clay pots is likely to change. As water evaporates from the sides, it leaves behind mineral deposits, creating a whitish crust. And in shady, moist sites, algae and mosses can grow on the clay, adding shades of green. Some gardeners love the appearance of aged clay, but if you prefer the new look, give your clay pots a good cleaning after you empty out the potting soil and before you put them away for the winter. First, use a scrub brush and soapy water to clean off any loose dirt and debris. Soak smaller pots overnight in a vinegar solution (1 part vinegar to 3 or 4 parts water), then scrub them again and rinse in clean water. On larger pots, spot-treat mineral stains with straight vinegar or a paste of baking soda and water, then scrub with a stiff brush, steel wool, or fine sandpaper.

The Versatile
PLASTIC POT

PLASTIC POTS AREN'T SOMETHING YOU JUST have to settle for if you're on a budget; they have many advantages beyond simply being inexpensive and easy to find. Plastic containers come in a wide range of colors, styles, and finishes, for instance, and their relatively light weight makes it easy to lift and move them. Granted, that can make smaller plastic pots prone to getting blown or knocked over in windy or high-traffic sites, but at least you don't have to worry about them breaking. And, the reduced weight is a big plus when you want to work with medium-sized and large containers, like this broad bowl planter. Its neutral gray color lets the colorful flowers and leaves be the stars — and by midsummer, you don't see much of the container anyway.

FULL SUN

CONTAINER: 24" WIDE × 8" HIGH

PLANTS:

1 BREATHLESS BLUSH spurge (*Euphorbia hypericifolia* 'Balreblus')

2 ELECTRIC PINK cordyline (*Cordyline banksii* 'Sprilecpink')

3 'Graffiti Rose' starflower (*Pentas lanceolata*)

4 'Harmony Snow' New Guinea impatiens (*Impatiens hawkeri*)

5 'Topaz Pink' fanflower (*Scaevola aemula*)

If you'd like to use a plastic pot or planter in an exposed, windy site, or where people and pets tend to congregate, low, broad shapes are a better choice than tall, narrow ones.

1. BREATHLESS BLUSH SPURGE

Euphorbia hypericifolia 'Balreblus' | one 4- to 6-inch pot

ALTERNATES: **DIAMOND FROST** ('Inneuphe') spurge or another 10- to 18-inch-tall, bushy plant with white flowers, such as Mexican fleabane (*Erigeron karvinskianus*) or white heliotrope (*Heliotropium arborescens* 'Alba')

2. ELECTRIC PINK CORDYLINE

Cordyline banksii 'Sprilecpink' | one 6- to 8-inch pot

ALTERNATES: **FESTIVAL RASPBERRY** ('Corbzr01') cordyline or another 18- to 24-inch-tall plant with spiky, pink-marked leaves, such as 'Fireworks' fountain grass (*Pennisetum setaceum*), 'Pink Stripe' New Zealand flax (*Phormium*), or tricolor Madagascar dragon tree (*Dracaena marginata* 'Tricolor')

4. 'HARMONY SNOW' NEW GUINEA IMPATIENS

Impatiens hawkeri | one 3- to 4-inch pot

ALTERNATES: **SUNPATIENS COMPACT WHITE IMPROVED** ('Sakimp027'), 'Florific White' or another white New Guinea impatiens, or another 10- to 18-inch-tall, bushy plant with relatively large, white flowers, such as 'Crystal White' zinnia (*Zinnia angustifolia*) or 'Pacifica White' rose periwinkle (*Catharanthus roseus*)

3. 'GRAFFITI ROSE' STARFLOWER

Pentas lanceolata
four 3- to 4-inch pots

ALTERNATES: 'Graffiti Pink' starflower or another 12- to 18-inch-tall, bushy plant with pink flowers, such as 'Archangel Pink' angelonia (*Angelonia angustifolia*) or 'Raspberry Nectar' hummingbird mint (*Agastache*)

5. 'TOPAZ PINK' FANFLOWER

Scaevola aemula
two 3- to 4-inch pots

ALTERNATES: 'Bombay Pink' fanflower or another 6- to 12-inch-tall, trailing plant with pink flowers or foliage, such as 'Blushing Bride' spiderwort (*Tradescantia*), 'Scopia Great Pink Ring' bacopa (*Sutera cordata*), or 'Twister Pink' verbena (*Verbena*)

THE VERSATILE PLASTIC POT

season by season

SPRING

ELECTRIC PINK cordyline is the star of this container right from the start, thanks to the bright pink striping on its spiky, burgundy foliage. The dark color in the cordyline leaves is repeated by deep purple shading in the center of the **BREATHLESS BLUSH** spurge leaves. You may also get a few hints of the complete color theme to come, if there are some early blooms on the other plants.

Chilly temperatures may stunt the growth of these plants, so hold off on planting until nighttime temperatures are at least 60°F/15°C. Water thoroughly once the plants are in place to settle them into the potting soil.

EARLY TO MID SUMMER

This container might look a little sparse right after planting, but as the weather warms up, they'll fill out quickly and begin flowering freely. Echoing the rosy stripes of **ELECTRIC PINK** cordyline are the first bright blooms on 'Graffiti Rose' starflower and softer 'Topaz Pink' fanflower, as well as the airy white blossoms of **BREATHLESS BLUSH** spurge and brilliant white 'Harmony Snow' New Guinea impatiens.

A shallow bowl planter like this can dry out quickly, so water it regularly if rain is lacking. Apply a liquid fertilizer every 7 to 10 days as well, to support all the new growth.

TIDBITS TIPS AND TRICKS

THE RIGHT PLANTS FOR PLASTIC. Because their sides aren't porous, like clay or wood, plastic containers dry out much more slowly, so they tend to need less frequent watering. If you're planning to use them for plants that prefer to be a bit on the drier side, such as salvias and succulents, make sure that there are multiple holes in the bottom, and use a potting mix with added perlite or grit so excess water drains out quickly. Or, save your plastic pots for plants that prefer to be evenly moist, like dahlias (*Dahlia*), impatiens (*Impatiens*), and ferns, or for sites that are exposed to lots of heat and sun, such as on a sunny deck or patio.

MID TO LATE SUMMER

This beautiful bowl is a confection in pink and white by now, with the spiky leaves of **ELECTRIC PINK** cordyline rising out of a cloud of both delicate and bold blooms.

Pay particularly careful attention to watering at this time of year — especially if the weather is very hot and/or windy — so the potting soil doesn't completely dry out. Keep up with fertilizing, too, so the flowering plants continue to produce new buds and blooms. Most of the blossoms will neatly drop off the plants as they finish; pick off any discolored petals or dead or damaged leaves. Clip back any especially long stems on the fanflower to encourage them to branch out and produce more flowers.

FALL

The flower-full show goes on well into fall — until frost zaps the plants, at least. That's a long season of interest from just five plants.

Keep watering and grooming your container as long as it looks good. Covering the plants with a sheet overnight may help to get this collection through a few light frosts. Once they get nipped by chilly weather, pull out the spurge, starflower, New Guinea impatiens, and fanflower and put them in your compost pile. If you have the room, it's worth trying to keep the cordyline for next year: pot it up and keep it in a bright, frost-free place for the winter.

POLISHING UP PLASTIC. Most plastic pots will last for at least a few years, even if you leave them outside all year round, but they'll stay in good shape longer if you bring them into a sheltered spot in the winter. When they start to look dull and dirty, use them as liners inside larger decorative pots. Or, scrub them with soap and water, rough up the surface a bit with steel wool or fine sandpaper, wipe off the dust, and then spruce them up with a spray paint meant for plastic. Your old plastic planters will look brand new in minutes.

COPPER *Beauty*

METAL CONTAINERS TEND TO LAST MANY years, and — unlike many types of containers — they can stay outside all winter without cracking as long as there are plenty of drainage holes. Cast iron is expensive and heavy but long-lasting, with a classic appearance well suited to formal settings, while steel and aluminum containers — in a range of weights and prices, with colorful powder coatings or shiny metallic finishes — tend to have a more contemporary look. This copper-finished planter holds a combination of orange, gold, bronzy purple, and green hues that harmonize well with its weathered finish.

PARTIAL TO FULL SHADE

CONTAINER: 15" WIDE × 18" HIGH

PLANTS:

1 'Amazon Mist' New Zealand hair sedge (*Carex comans*)

2 Golden Makino stonecrop (*Sedum makinoi* 'Ogon')

3 'Orange Marmalade' firecracker flower (*Crossandra infundibuliformis*)

4 'Prince of Orange' philodendron (*Philodendron*)

5 'Sparks Will Fly' begonia (*Begonia*)

Aged or shiny copper containers tend to be pricey but are undeniably elegant, and their colors complement many plants.

1. 'AMAZON MIST' NEW ZEALAND HAIR SEDGE

Carex comans | one 4-inch pot

ALTERNATES: 'Bronzita' New Zealand hair sedge or another 10- to 18-inch-tall, upright or mounded plant with arching or spiky, pale green, bronzy, gray-blue, or yellow leaves, such as 'Blue Zinger' blue sedge (*Carex flacca*) or 'All Gold' Hakone grass (*Hakonechloa macra*)

2. GOLDEN MAKINO STONECROP

Sedum makinoi 'Ogon' one 4-inch pot

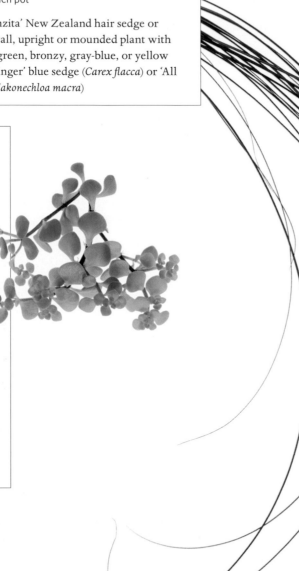

ALTERNATES: Another 2- to 6-inch-tall, trailing plant with yellow, yellow-and-green, or orangey foliage, such as 'Beedham's White' spotted deadnettle (*Lamium maculatum*), 'Illumination' lesser periwinkle (*Vinca minor*), or 'Redstone Falls' or 'Yellowstone Falls' foamy bells (×*Heucherella*)

3. 'ORANGE MARMALADE' FIRECRACKER FLOWER

Crossandra infundibuliformis | one 4-inch pot

ALTERNATES: Another 8- to 12-inch-tall, upright plant with orange or yellow flowers or yellow-variegated leaves, such as croton (*Codiaeum variegatum* var. *pictum*), 'Jungle Gold' impatiens (*Impatiens auricoma*), or shrimp plant (*Justicia brandegeana*)

5. 'SPARKS WILL FLY' BEGONIA

Begonia
one 3- to 4-inch pot

ALTERNATES:
'Orange Rubra' begonia, 'Nonstop Mocca Deep Orange' tuberous begonia (*Begonia* × *tuberhybrida*), Sutherland's begonia (*B. sutherlandii*), or another 6- to 10-inch-tall, bushy plant with orange flowers or with dark foliage, such as 'Catlin's Giant' or 'Jungle Beauty' ajuga (*Ajuga reptans*)

4. 'PRINCE OF ORANGE' PHILODENDRON

Philodendron | one 4-inch pot

ALTERNATES: 'Autumn' philodendron or another mounded to upright, 8- to 18-inch-tall plant with broad or ferny, orangey leaves, such as 'Brilliantissima' autumn fern (*Dryopteris erythrosora*), 'ColorBlaze Keystone Kopper' coleus (*Solenostemon scutellarioides*), or 'Southern Comfort' heuchera (*Heuchera*)

COPPER BEAUTY

season by season

SPRING

Early-season impact in this container comes almost entirely from lovely leaves: gracefully arching, pale green 'Amazon Mist' New Zealand hair sedge; succulent yellow-golden Makino stonecrop; shiny, bright and deep green 'Orange Marmalade' firecracker flower; glossy, coppery orange 'Prince of Orange' philodendron; and green-veined, bronzy purple 'Sparks Will Fly' begonia.

Several of these plants are very cold-sensitive — especially the firecracker flower and philodendron, which really want temperatures that are consistently above 60°F/15°C, at least — so don't be in a hurry to plant until the weather is dependably warm, even if that's not until very late spring. Water after planting to settle the potting soil around the roots.

EARLY TO MID SUMMER

Joining the coppers, bronzes, golds, and greens of the various leaves now are the first flowers: bright orange blossoms in dense spikes on 'Orange Marmalade' firecracker flower and nodding sprays on 'Sparks Will Fly' begonia. Golden Makino sedum blooms, too, but you'll hardly notice the yellow flowers against the yellow foliage.

Water as needed to keep the potting soil evenly moist; these plants don't like to be constantly soggy, but they really don't like to dry out, either. Apply a liquid fertilizer every 10 to 14 days to encourage steady growth.

TIDBITS TIPS AND TRICKS

CREATIVE METAL POTS. If you can't find metal planters you like where you usually buy pots, look around for other metal containers that you can repurpose for your garden. Home-improvement stores, for instance, usually carry empty paint cans and scrub buckets that are perfectly sized to hold single or multiple small plants. Farm-supply stores offer a wealth of galvanized metal items that make out-of-the-ordinary planters, from small chicken feeders and waterers to sizable tubs and tanks meant for larger livestock. Yard sales and thrift shops can provide a wealth of other whimsical options, such as old metal wagons, coolers, kettles, or cooking pots. Before planting in metal containers meant for other purposes, use a large nail or a drill with a bit meant for metal to add lots of drainage holes to the base. Or, use them for water gardens.

HEAT PROTECTION. From your plants' perspective, there's one main drawback to metal: it heats up and cools down quickly, subjecting roots that are near the sides to damaging temperature extremes. To provide a bit of insulation, line the sides with bubble

The orange flowers of 'Orange Marmalade' fire-cracker flower and 'Sparks Will Fly' begonia are most likely to first catch your eye at this point, but the various foliage shapes, colors, and textures still contribute significant interest to this metallic container later in the summer. There will likely also be some yellow flowers on the golden Makino sedum.

Continue watering and fertilizing regularly, and pinch or snip off any dead or discolored leaves and any dead flowers as you spot them to keep the plants looking their best. You may also need to clip back the longest stems on the firecracker flower and the begonia by about half to keep them in proportion to the rest of the container. You might also want to occasionally cut off a few of the oldest leaves on the philodendron: they can get quite large and crowd out the other plants.

Golden Makino sedum is generally done flowering well before early fall, but 'Orange Marmalade' firecracker flower and 'Sparks Will Fly' begonia keep blooming into autumn, complemented by the various forms of beautiful foliage and usually lasting until the first frost.

Keep watering while the plants continue to look good. Leave the container in place until cold kills the tender plants, if you want to get the longest possible display, or take it apart in early fall. The New Zealand hair sedge and golden Makino sedum should be winter-hardy in Zone 7 and warmer areas; elsewhere, you could pot them up and keep them in a cool, bright spot for the winter. Pot up the firecracker flower, begonia, and philodendron (or take cuttings of the first two) and keep them in a warm, bright place to enjoy them as winter houseplants.

wrap or sheets of Styrofoam before adding the potting soil and planting. Or, plant your combination in a slightly smaller pot and slip it into the metal one, so there's a bit of space between the walls of the two containers. Or, keep your metal planters in shady spots so they're not exposed to direct sun.

METAL UPKEEP. Metal containers that start out bright and shiny tend to dull, darken, or rust quickly once you expose them to outdoor conditions. On some metals, like copper, the patina creates a handsome aged look; on others, it may just appear tired and neglected. To keep the shiny look, use an exterior clear-coat sealant before adding the potting soil; re-treat the container every year with the coating. If there's already some staining or oxidation, remove it with steel wool or fine sandpaper before using the clear sealant, or use exterior paint to freshen up the appearance.

CEMENTED *in* PLACE

WEIGHT IS ONE OF THE MOST DISTINCTIVE characteristics of cement planters, making them a good choice for windy or high-traffic sites where lighter containers might easily get blown or knocked over. Their thick sides make them super-durable and also help to insulate tender roots from both extreme heat and freezing temperatures. Cement pots are more than just heavy, though: they also give you a wide range of shape options, color choices, and surface finishes that range from smooth and even to rough and weathered. This natural-gray planter houses a collection of small-scale clumping and creeping perennials in shades of green and yellow to brighten a shady spot.

PARTIAL TO FULL SHADE

CONTAINER: 15" WIDE × 12" HIGH

PLANTS:

1 'Fire Island' hosta (*Hosta*)

2 Miniature golden sweet flag (*Acorus gramineus* 'Minimus Aureus')

3 Golden spikemoss (*Selaginella kraussiana* 'Aurea')

4 'Gyoku-ryu' mondo grass (*Ophiopogon japonicus*)

5 Corsican mint (*Mentha requienii*)

Light gray is the most common color for cement containers, but you can also find them colored with pigments to produce shades of tan, brick red, or even mossy green.

THE 5-PLANT PALETTE

2. MINIATURE GOLDEN SWEET FLAG

Acorus gramineus 'Minimus Aureus' one 4-inch pot

ALTERNATES: Another 2- to 4-inch-tall, spiky or mounded perennial with yellow, yellow-and-green, or solid green leaves, such as European wild ginger (*Asarum europaeum*), strawberry begonia (*Saxifraga stolonifera*), or wintergreen (*Gaultheria procumbens*)

1. 'FIRE ISLAND' HOSTA

Hosta | one 4-inch pot

ALTERNATES: 'Maui Buttercup', 'Paradise Island', 'Prairie Moon', or another small hosta with solid yellow or yellow-variegated leaves, or another 4- to 8-inch-tall, mounded perennial in the same color range, such as 'Citronelle' or 'Electra' heuchera (*Heuchera*)

3. GOLDEN SPIKEMOSS

Selaginella kraussiana 'Aurea' | one 4-inch pot

ALTERNATES: Another 1- to 2-inch-tall, creeping, yellow-leaved perennial, such as golden Makino stonecrop (*Sedum makinoi* 'Ogon') or Scotch moss (*Sagina subulata* 'Aurea')

4. 'GYOKU-RYU' MONDO GRASS

Ophiopogon japonicus | four 2-inch pots

ALTERNATES: 'Kyoto Dwarf' or dwarf ('Nana') mondo grass, or another 2- to 4-inch-tall, rosette-forming perennial with rich green leaves, such as 'Emerald Chip' or 'Pink Elf' ajuga (*Ajuga reptans*)

5. CORSICAN MINT

Mentha requienii | one 4-inch pot

ALTERNATES: Another ½- to 1-inch-tall, green-leaved, creeping plant, such as baby's tears (*Soleirolia soleirolii*) or miniature moneywort (*Lysimachia japonica* 'Minutissima')

CEMENTED IN PLACE
season by season

SPRING

This collection of diminutive perennials looks charming right from day one, thanks to the various shades of green and yellow in the foliage and the touch of red from the hosta stems. The contrasting plant forms (from mounded to creeping to vase shaped to tufted), foliage shapes (from broad to ferny to spiky), and range of leaf sizes add extra elements of interest for a pretty spring display.

These five perennials are all relatively cold-tolerant, so you can get this container started as soon as you get the plants. Just keep in mind that if you're starting with a hosta plant that was kept in a greenhouse, wait until all danger of frost has passed to set it outside. At planting time, first settle the hosta, miniature golden sweet flag, golden spikemoss, and mondo grasses into the potting soil. Then, remove the Corsican mint from the pot you bought it in, use a pair of garden scissors to cut it into four parts, and plug those smaller pieces into the empty spaces.

EARLY TO MID SUMMER

Leaf colors continue to add the main interest to this classic cement pedestal planter through the summer. 'Fire Island' hosta, miniature golden sweet flag, and golden spikemoss typically have the brightest yellow on their new leaves, aging to more of a greenish yellow (the more shade, the more obvious the green). The extra-dark green of 'Gyoku-ryu' mondo grass and bright green of the Corsican mint complement the range of yellows, with an extra touch of color from the red blush on the leaf stems of the hosta. You'll probably see some flowers, too: tiny purplish pink blossoms on the Corsican mint, small pale lavender bells on the mondo grass, and reddish stems with purple trumpets on the hosta. The miniature golden sweet flag might produce tiny tan flowers in early summer, but you probably won't notice them.

There's little maintenance to do with this container, other than regular watering and applying a dose of liquid fertilizer once or twice a month.

TIDBITS TIPS AND TRICKS

MAKE-YOUR-OWN PLANTERS. The weight of cement planters can make it a challenge to get them home and then move them once they're there. If you like the look and durability of cement but need something that's easier to move, look for planters that are made from cement mixed with fiberglass. Or, buy a bag of cement at your local home-improvement store and make your own planters at home. Use the cement as it is (just add water to the powder) or customize the mix with pigments to change the color and additives, such as vermiculite, to reduce the weight and/or add texture. You can find many different recipes by searching the Web for phrases such as "make a cement planter," "make your own concrete planter," or "make a hypertufa planter." ("Hypertufa" is a catchall term for planters made from cement mixed with materials such as sand, peat moss, and perlite to create a rocklike appearance.)

All of the wonderful foliage features from earlier in the growing season continue through the summer season, along with the potential for a few more flowers on the Corsican mint, mondo grass, and hosta.

Be sure to keep up with regular watering so the potting soil doesn't dry out (the miniature golden sweet flag, in particular, is likely to develop brown leaf tips if that happens). Corsican mint spreads quickly and may start creeping over the mondo grass; if that happens, snip out some of the mint shoots so the mondo grass doesn't get smothered. If the hosta flowers, clip off the bloom stalks at their base once the blossoms are finished.

The lovely leaves in this cement planter continue to shine well until fall — at least until frost nips the leaves of the hosta.

Continue to water the plants while they're still growing. Once the hosta is finished (or earlier, if you wish), you'll want to dismantle the collection so you can bring the emptied planter into a sheltered spot for the winter. Transplant the hosta to your garden (it should be fine outside in Zones 3 to 9). South of Zone 6, you could plant out the other perennials as well; elsewhere, pot them up individually, put them in a bright spot indoors, and enjoy them as houseplants for the winter.

WINTER PROTECTION. Cement planters are amazingly durable, but they *can* crack if left outside for the winter. Moist potting soil will expand as it freezes, exerting tremendous amounts of force on the sides of the container and causing them to break. Moisture within the walls of the pots can also cause damage as the water freezes and thaws. The best protection is to bring concrete pieces into a shed or garage for the winter, but that can be tough with bigger pots. Applying a clear concrete sealer to all sides of each pot every few years can help to prevent some damage; so can setting them up on blocks or strips of wood for the winter, to ensure water will drain out. Even better, remove the potting soil in fall, turn the pots over, set them on wood strips or bricks so they're not resting directly on the soil, and cover them with burlap and plastic.

Country HARDWOOD

FROM ROUGH, RUSTIC HALF-BARRELS TO finely finished hardwood planters, containers crafted from wood are a wonderful choice for gardeners who appreciate natural materials. They're also terrific from a plant's perspective, because the porous sides readily allow air to reach the roots, encouraging excellent growth, and their thickness provides a measure of protection from both heat and cold. Wooden planters come in a wide range of prices, based on what they're made from. Pine tends to be inexpensive but may last only a few years; naturally rot-resistant woods, such as cedar and cypress, last longer but can be very expensive. This hardwood planter contains a collection of colorful and fragrant foliage that would look lovely on a backyard deck or patio.

FULL SUN TO PARTIAL SHADE

CONTAINER: 18" LONG × 18" WIDE × 20" HIGH

PLANTS:

1 CALIENTE FIRE geranium (*Pelargonium* 'Cante Fir09')

2 'ColorBlaze Keystone Kopper' coleus (*Solenostemon scutellarioides*)

3 'Golden Delicious' pineapple sage (*Salvia elegans*)

4 'Little Ruby' alternanthera (*Alternanthera dentata*)

5 Peppermint geranium (*Pelargonium tomentosum*)

1. CALIENTE FIRE GERANIUM

Pelargonium 'Cante Fir09'
one 4- to 6-inch pot

ALTERNATES:
Another 8- to 18-inch-tall,
bushy to semi-trailing
plant with green leaves
and red flowers, such
as 'Empress of India'
nasturtium (*Tropaeolum
majus*), **SUNPATIENS
COMPACT RED**
impatiens (*Impatiens*
'Sakimp024'), or 'Santa
Cruz Sunset' begonia
(*Begonia boliviensis*)

**2. 'COLORBLAZE
KEYSTONE
KOPPER'
COLEUS**

Solenostemon scutellarioides
one 4- to 6-inch pot

ALTERNATES:
'ColorBlaze Sedona'
coleus or another 8- to
18-inch-tall, bushy to semi-
trailing plant with orangey
to coppery foliage, such
as 'Southern Comfort'
heuchera (*Heuchera*) or
'Toffee Twist' sedge (*Carex
flagellifera*)

3. 'GOLDEN DELICIOUS' PINEAPPLE SAGE

Salvia elegans
one 4- to 6-inch pot

ALTERNATES: Another 2- to 3-foot-tall, bushy or spiky plant with yellow or yellow-and-green foliage, such as golden bay (*Laurus nobilis* 'Aurea'), 'Yellow Wave' New Zealand flax (*Phormium*), or sanchezia (*Sanchezia speciosa*)

4. 'LITTLE RUBY' ALTERNANTHERA

Alternanthera dentata | one 4- to 6-inch pot

ALTERNATES: Another 8- to 18-inch-tall, bushy to semi-trailing plant with deep purple or red leaves, such as 'Red Threads' Joseph's coat (*Alternanthera ficoidea*), 'Purple Lady' bloodleaf (*Iresine herbstii*), or 'Purple Ruffles' basil (*Ocimum basilicum*)

5. PEPPERMINT GERANIUM

Pelargonium tomentosum | one 4- to 6-inch pot

ALTERNATES: Another 6- to 12-inch-tall, bushy or trailing plant with broad, lacy, or frilly, rich green leaves, such as **ILLUSION GARNET LACE** sweet potato vine (*Ipomoea batatas* 'Ncornsp013gnlc') or 'Triple Curled' parsley (*Petroselinum crispum* var. *crispum*)

SPRING

The intense foliage colors of these plants — rich greens from the **CALIENTE FIRE** and peppermint geraniums, coppery orange from the 'ColorBlaze Keystone Kopper' coleus, deep purple from 'Little Ruby' alternanthera, and bright yellow from 'Golden Delicious' pineapple sage — make for a container that's eye-catching right from the start. You'll also experience the extra-special fragrance factor right away: as you handle the plants, they'll release the fruity scent of pineapple sage and the minty goodness of peppermint geranium.

Don't be in a hurry to get this container planted in spring, because these plants tend to be touchy about cold temperatures, especially if they've just come out of a warm greenhouse. Wait until nighttime temperatures consistently stay above 55°F/13°C and the plants are adapted to outdoor conditions. Water after planting to settle the potting soil and get the plants off to a good start.

EARLY TO MID SUMMER

Lovely leaves are still the main focus of this planter: most obviously for their colors but also for their scents, so don't forget to gently rub the leaves of the 'Golden Delicious' pineapple sage and peppermint geranium as you pass by. **CALIENTE FIRE** geranium starts to add sparks of rich red from its dainty flowers now, too.

There's not much to do to your container now: just water as needed to keep the potting soil evenly moist, and apply a liquid fertilizer every 10 to 14 days to support steady growth.

TIDBITS TIPS AND TRICKS

ENVIRONMENTALLY CONSCIOUS LUMBER. "Rot-resistant" woods are often a selling point for higher-end containers, but it's important to do a bit of research before you buy, because some of these materials, such as nyatoh and old-growth redwood, may be harvested from environmentally sensitive areas. Some manufacturers claim that their planters are more environmentally friendly because they're made from "plantation-grown" wood; however, that may not be a better choice if those plantations were created by clearing native forest to plant timber species. If you are concerned about using environmentally sound materials in your garden, look for planters made from reused or reclaimed lumber, or from lumber that's certified to be from sustainably managed forests by an independent oversight organization, such as the Forest Stewardship Council (FSC).

MID TO LATE SUMMER

The lush leaves look beautiful through the rest of the summer as the plants continue to fill out and mingle their stems, with the added bonus of the intense red **CALIENTE FIRE** geranium flowers.

Be sure to keep up with watering, especially in hot or windy conditions, because the abundance of leaves can lose a lot of water quickly. Continue to use a liquid fertilizer every 10 to 14 days. Every week or two, take a few minutes to clip out any dead, damaged, or discolored leaves, as well as any finished flower stems on the **CALIENTE FIRE** geranium. Pinch off any flower buds that form at the shoot tips of the coleus. Take a good look at the overall balance of the container and cut out some of the large leaves or even entire shoots of the peppermint geranium and pineapple sage to keep them from crowding out or overgrowing their companions.

FALL

The foliage continues to look fabulous into early fall, at least, and so do the **CALIENTE FIRE** geranium's red flowers, joined now by sprays of scarlet blooms on the 'Golden Delicious' pineapple sage.

Keep watering as long as the plants are still growing. If you want to keep some or all of them for next year, take cuttings in early fall, pot them up, and overwinter them in a warm, bright place. When frost calls a halt to the growing season, pull out and compost all of the plants.

FINISHING TOUCHES. Left untreated, wood planters will change color over time, eventually developing a silvery or gray patina. If you wish to keep the natural wood look, with a visible grain, consider a clear sealant meant for outdoor use, such as an exterior varnish (also called spar varnish) or a clear penetrating exterior oil, such as tung oil. If you want to change the color to match your home or your favorite plants, use an acrylic or oil-based paint or stain. Strong sun, moisture, and extreme temperatures can be tough on wood finishes, so keep in mind that you'll need to reapply whatever finish you choose every few years (or maybe even more frequently) to keep your planter looking its best.

Eye-Catching CERAMIC

GLAZED POTS ARE AMONG THE MOST distinctive and colorful of container choices. Also commonly known as ceramic pots, they are clay pots that are dipped, brushed, or sprayed with a mixture of minerals and exposed to heat to melt the glaze into a coating. Glazed pots may have a dull finish but are usually shiny, with a hard, glasslike finish. This five-plant collection includes soft colors to complement the light green and cream colors of the container, and bushy and upright plants, so they don't cover up the interesting glaze pattern.

FULL SUN TO PARTIAL SHADE

CONTAINER: 15" WIDE × 15" HIGH

PLANTS:

1 'Ellwoodii' Lawson false cypress (*Chamaecyparis lawsoniana*)

2 Variegated hebe (*Hebe speciosa* 'Variegata')

3 'Silver Dust' dusty miller (*Senecio cineraria*)

4 'First Yellow' zonal geranium (*Pelargonium* × *hortorum*)

5 MILLION BELLS BOUQUET CREAM calibrachoa (*Calibrachoa* 'Suncallemon')

Glazed pots can be very
heavy, so it's smart to place
the container in the spot
where you plan to keep it all
through the growing season
before you fill it.

THE 5-PLANT PALETTE

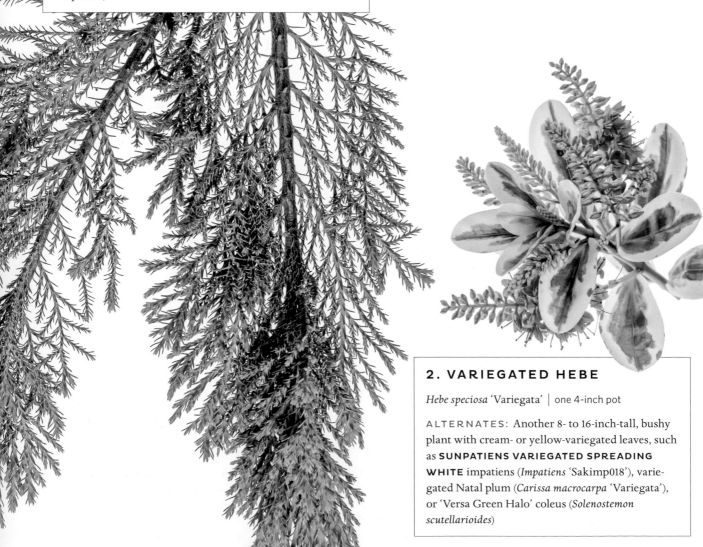

1. 'ELLWOODII' LAWSON FALSE CYPRESS

Chamaecyparis lawsoniana │ one 8-inch pot

ALTERNATES: 'Blue Surprise' Lawson false cypress or another 18- to 30-inch-tall, distinctly upright or spiky plant with silvery blue or gray-blue foliage, such as 'Blue Arrow' juniper (*Juniperus virginiana*), silver spear (*Astelia chathamica*), or 'Prairie Blues' little bluestem (*Schizachyrium scoparium*)

2. VARIEGATED HEBE

Hebe speciosa 'Variegata' │ one 4-inch pot

ALTERNATES: Another 8- to 16-inch-tall, bushy plant with cream- or yellow-variegated leaves, such as **SUNPATIENS VARIEGATED SPREADING WHITE** impatiens (*Impatiens* 'Sakimp018'), variegated Natal plum (*Carissa macrocarpa* 'Variegata'), or 'Versa Green Halo' coleus (*Solenostemon scutellarioides*)

3. 'SILVER DUST' DUSTY MILLER

Senecio cineraria | two 4-inch pots

ALTERNATES: Another 8- to 16-inch-tall, bushy plant with gray or silvery leaves, such as 'Berggarten' culinary sage (*Salvia officinalis*), 'Icicles' silver spike (*Helichrysum thianshanicum*), or curry plant (*Helichrysum angustifolium*)

4. 'FIRST YELLOW' ZONAL GERANIUM

Pelargonium × hortorum one 4-inch pot

ALTERNATES: Another 6- to 10-inch-tall, bushy plant with white, cream, or soft yellow flowers, such as LITTLE LUCKY LEMON CREAM lantana (*Lantana camara* 'Ballucream') or DIAMOND FROST spurge (*Euphorbia hypericifolia* 'Inneuphe')

5. MILLION BELLS BOUQUET CREAM CALIBRACHOA

Calibrachoa 'Suncallemon' | one 4-inch pot

ALTERNATES: Another 6- to 10-inch-tall, bushy or semi-trailing plant with cream or yellow flowers, such as SURFINIA PATIO YELLOW petunia (*Petunia* 'Sunpatiki') or 'Milkmaid' nasturtium (*Tropaeolum majus*)

EYE-CATCHING CERAMIC
season by season

Expect practically instant impact from this collection, right from planting time. The icy blue foliage and narrowly upright form of the 'Ellwoodii' Lawson false cypress creates a dramatic center accent, skirted in shades of green and cream from the multicolored leaves of variegated hebe and the dainty blooms of 'First Yellow' geranium. **MILLION BELLS BOUQUET CREAM** calibrachoa will likely already have a few flowers now, too, and 'Silver Dust' dusty miller offers a perfect finishing touch with its deeply lobed, silvery leaves.

Get this container started any time after all danger of frost has passed. Add the plants, then water to settle them into the potting soil.

All the lovely features of this collection that you enjoyed since planting continue into summer. The featured foliage — blue 'Ellwoodii' Lawson false cypress, cream-and-green variegated hebe, and silvery white 'Silver Dust' dusty miller — provides no-trouble color and textural interest through this period. The companion flowers add their share to the show with new, light yellow blooms continually appearing on the 'First Yellow' geranium and **MILLION BELLS BOUQUET CREAM** calibrachoa. The addition of purple flower spikes of the variegated hebe around this time is a wonderful bonus.

Water regularly when rain is lacking, so the potting soil doesn't completely dry out, and use a liquid fertilizer every 10 to 14 days to encourage flowering. Other than keeping the geranium flower clusters picked off as they turn brown, there's little you need to do now to keep this container in prime condition.

TIDBITS TIPS AND TRICKS

TYPES OF GLAZE. The quality and treatment of the clay, the type of glaze used, and the amount of heat used to "fire" the finished pieces all affect the price and longevity of glazed pots. Those fired at lower temperatures — sometimes called glazed earthenware — tend to be inexpensive but are likely to crack or crumble if exposed to freezing temperatures. Those fired at higher temperatures — usually referred to as glazed stoneware — tend to be more durable but may still be damaged in winter. To minimize the need to move your glazed pots indoors for the winter, look for those labeled "frost-resistant" or "freeze-resistant." Keep in mind, though, that after several years, even these may be susceptible to cracking.

MID TO LATE SUMMER

The cool colors of this glazed container continue to provide a refreshing sight through the heat of the summer as the various green, blue, and silvery leaves and pale-tinted petals keep going, often accented with a few additional purple spikes on the hebe.

Keep up with regular watering through this period, and continue to fertilize through midsummer. Clip off the geranium and hebe flower clusters as they drop their petals or turn brown to keep the plants looking fresh and possibly encourage more blossoms. If the calibrachoa is looking a bit straggly or not blooming as freely now, cut the stems back by about half; it should be bushier and flowering well again by the end of the summer. Snip off some shoots of the dusty miller and hebe as needed to keep them well shaped and prevent them from crowding out their companions. The Lawson false cypress might spread out a bit as the season progresses. If you want to keep it more narrowly upright, give it a few loose wraps of monofilament fishing line or black or gray string to pull the sides together.

FALL

This mix of flowers and foliage should look good through early fall — until the first frost, at least. And if you drape a sheet over the plants on frosty nights to protect them from chilly temperatures, you'll probably be able to get extra days or even weeks of beauty.

Continue watering the plants as long as they look good. In frost-free areas, leave the container in place to enjoy the pot and plants well into winter. Elsewhere, plan on dismantling the container before freezing temperatures arrive. Transplant the Lawson false cypress to your garden in Zones 6 to 9 (it's usually hardy to Zone 5 but may not make it through the winter there from a mid-fall planting). Or, leave it in the pot and bring it into a cool, bright place, such as an enclosed but unheated porch, for the winter. Move the geranium and hebe to individual pots and enjoy them as houseplants, if you want to keep them for next year, or discard them. It's possible to keep the dusty miller and calibrachoa that way, too, but it's usually easier to discard them (in your compost pile) and buy new plants next year.

THE IMPORTANCE OF HOLES. It's extremely difficult to add drainage holes to glazed pots, so make sure they have at least one hole — preferably several — before you buy them. If you fall in love with a glazed pot that doesn't have drainage, consider using it as a "cachepot": plant your combination in a clay or plastic pot that will fit inside the ceramic one, then remember to lift out the plastic pot regularly and dump out any water that has accumulated in the bottom of the ceramic one. Or, use it for a container water garden.

INDEX

Page numbers in *italic* indicate photos.

OTHER BOOKS BY
Nancy J. Ondra

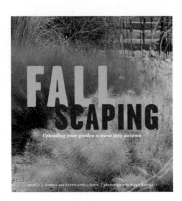

FALLSCAPING
A comprehensive guide to the best plants for
brightening late-season landscapes.
240 pages. Paper with flaps.
ISBN 978-1-58017-680-4.

FIVE-PLANT GARDENS
Illustrated garden plans and season-by-season
growing highlights for 52 perennial gardens,
each one featuring just five plants.
184 pages. Paper. ISBN 978-1-61212-004-1.

GRASSES
Photographs and plans for 20 gardens that
highlight the beauty of grasses in combination
with perennials, annuals, and shrubs.
144 pages. Paper with flaps.
ISBN 978-1-58017-423-7.

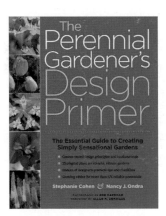

THE PERENNIAL GARDENER'S DESIGN PRIMER
A lively, authoritative guide to creating
perennial gardens using basic design principles
for putting plants together in pleasing
and practical ways.
320 pages. Paper. ISBN 978-1-58017-543-2.